The Art of Jewelry
Paper Jewelry

THE ART OF JEWELRY
PAPER
JEWELRY

35 CREATIVE PROJECTS

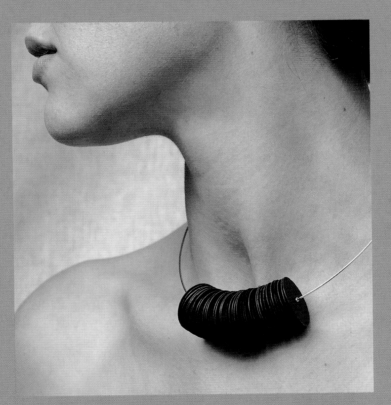

MARTHE LE VAN

LARK BOOKS

A Division of Sterling Publishing Co., Inc.
New York

EDITOR: VIVIAN ROTHE

ART DIRECTOR: DANA M. IRWIN

COVER DESIGNER: BARBARA ZARETSKY

ASSOCIATE EDITOR: NATHALIE MORNU

ASSOCIATE ART DIRECTOR: LANCE WILLE

ART PRODUCTION ASSISTANT: JEFF HAMILTON

EDITORIAL ASSISTANCE: DELORES GOSNELL,
DAWN DILLINGHAM

ILLUSTRATOR: OLIVIER ROLLIN

TEMPLATES: ORRIN LUNDGREN

PHOTOGRAPHER: STEWART O'SHIELDS

PROOFREADER: SHERRY HAMES

Library of Congress Cataloging-in-Publication Data

Le Van, Marthe.
  The art of jewelry : paper jewelry : 35 creative projects / Marthe Le Van.
      p. cm.
  Includes bibliographical references and index.
  ISBN 1-57990-814-4 (hardcover)
  1. Paper work.   2. Jewelry making. I. Title.
TT870.L335 2006
745.594'2--dc22

                                                                2006016109

10 9 8 7 6 5 4 3 2 1

First Edition

Published by Lark Books, A Division of
Sterling Publishing Co., Inc.
387 Park Avenue South, New York, N.Y. 10016

Text © 2006, Lark Books
Photography © 2006, Lark Books unless otherwise specified
Illustrations © 2006, Lark Books

Distributed in Canada by Sterling Publishing,
c/o Canadian Manda Group, 165 Dufferin Street
Toronto, Ontario, Canada M6K 3H6

Distributed in the United Kingdom by GMC Distribution Services,
Castle Place, 166 High Street, Lewes, East Sussex, England BN7 1XU

Distributed in Australia by Capricorn Link (Australia) Pty Ltd.,
P.O. Box 704, Windsor, NSW 2756 Australia

If you have questions or comments about this book, please contact:
Lark Books
67 Broadway
Asheville, NC 28801
(828) 253-0467

Manufactured in China

ISBN 13: 978-1-57990-814-0
ISBN 10: 1-57990-814-4

For information about custom editions, special sales, premium and
corporate purchases, please contact Sterling Sp
at 800-805-5489 or specialsales@sterlingpub.co

CONTENTS

INTRODUCTION

W

When you picture jewelry, you might conjure images of precious metals, faceted gemstones, painterly enamels, and strands of pearls. Paper may not even enter your mind. But just take a look at the imaginative creations featured in this book, and you will soon discover the beauty, versatility, and artistic appeal of paper jewelry.

Paper Jewelry is an extraordinary collection of 35 projects for you to make designed by some of today's leading jewelers. Collaged pendants, origami rings, sewn bracelets, and knitted necklaces are just a few of the fantastic forms you can create. Step-by-step instructions, gorgeous hand-sketched illustrations, and precise templates will guide you from start to finish. Sprinkled throughout is a large gallery of breath-taking and diverse images that is sure to inspire. Making paper jewelry is a process that everyone can enjoy, and you'll find the sensation of wearing your own one-of-a-kind creation to be absolutely exhilarating.

Consider the range of origami, displayed to perfection in Kelly Nye's *Origami Crane Cocktail Ring* and D. Lynn Reid's *Pinwheel Earrings*. Then move on to other types of paper folding, such as the splashy fun of Yael Friedman's paper diamond ring, and the rich textures of handmade lokta paper in Elizabeth Hake's *Accordion Pendant*. The classic qualities of folded vellum are used with distinction in K. Dana Kagrise's *Book-Stitched Bracelet* and Cynthia Wuller's *Ethereal Leaf Earrings*.

Expand your skills to work with jeweler's tools to cut, shape, and connect sheet metal, following Francine Haywood's methods to make the elegant *Vapor & Smoke Earrings*. Acrylic sheets can be used for jewelry making with an innovative effect as well, as evidenced by Dorothea Hosom's *Art of Geometry Brooch* and Elizabeth Hake's contemporary *Mulberry Bangles*.

Experience the glossy and long-lasting quality of laminated paper jewelry. James Bové's *Golden Paper Crystals*, Joanna Gollberg's *Blooming Charm Bracelet*, and Candie Cooper's *Nature-In-Paper Brooches* show the fascinating range of this paper technique. Or follow Marjorie Schick's methods to make a free-form papier-mâché necklace.

Creating a wire framework for tissue paper is used with fascinating effect in Joanna Gollberg's *Translucent Triangles Necklace*. The combination of contrasting textures is also the fundamental design of Carolina Tell's *Pearls & Cardboard Cuff*. Decoupage is used elegantly in Kyoko Urino's *Cherry Orb Necklace*.

Paper, which can have the qualities of fabric, lends itself to artistic stitching with interesting results, as seen in Francine Haywood's *French Knots & Crosses Necklace* and Elizabeth Hake's *Stuffed Pod Pendant*. Grace Willard changes paper from its usual sheet form to a cord, then creates a *Knitted Paper Necklace*.

The projects cover the gamut of in-fashion jewelry, from sophisticated designs for special occasions to casual, everyday wear. But each piece has one thing in common—all are a celebration of paper jewelry as art.

THE BASICS

PAPERS

Today's papers offer incredible variety: from plain, stiff kraft boards to wildly patterned and colorful sheets that mimic the pliability of soft woven cloth. Shop for paper in fine art supply and craft stores, as well as in home improvement stores, party and office supply stores, and from online suppliers. Recycled magazines and catalogs are another excellent source of paper; the free-form *Butterfly Brooch* (page 60) turns scrap and waste papers into a stunning piece of jewelry.

ART PAPERS

A wide variety of fine papers are made for use with art techniques, such as drawing and sketching, painting, or printing. These papers are made in a variety of weights (thicknesses), with smooth or textured surfaces, and a range of colors. Use them in their natural state or embellished with whatever techniques you desire.

TISSUE PAPERS & NAPKINS

Tissue manufacturers offer consumers stylish choices from simple white paper to contemporary patterns, from dazzling metallics to faux animal-skin prints. Tissue papers are an excellent choice for decoupage, as used in making the *Translucent Triangles Necklace* (page 50) and the *Decoupage Earrings & Bracelet* (page 70). Decorative double-ply napkins can be used with decoupage techniques, too. Cut out individual motifs, use the broad colorful borders, or incorporate the entire napkin in a variety of ways.

PAPER BOARDS

Single-face cardboard, sometimes called corrugated paper, is available in a variety of colors and flute sizes. (The flute is the rippled layer attached to or between the outer flat layers.) The color palette is not limited to the natural light-brown color. Today's choices range from solid pastels to bold primaries to metallic colors. You can modify their surfaces to create a striking piece of jewelry, such as the *Pearls & Cardboard Cuff* (page 32).

Double-wall cardboard, the common brown cardboard box, is made of single-face cardboard with an additional face. It's the workhorse of paper crafting. Use it to form three-dimensional shapes to cover with papier-mâché, or as a substitute cutting surface if you don't wish to invest in a cutting mat.

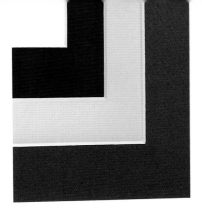

Poster board is a useful single-ply board that is lightweight, easily scored, inexpensive, and readily available. Manufacturers have responded to consumer tastes with fluorescent colors and metallic finishes, in addition to the traditional range of colors. Use it as a flat sheet or shape it into complex geometric shapes.

Illustration and mat boards are found in stores that stock fine art supplies. These strong, smooth-surfaced boards are available in a variety of thicknesses and colors. Store them flat at all times to prevent warping.

Foam-core board is made of two layers of smooth card stock laminated over a layer of polystyrene. White and black foam-core boards are commonly available in craft and office supply stores. You can't fold or crease this board, but it can be glued or pinned together to form three-dimensional shapes.

VELLUM

Delicate, translucent sheets of vellum are popular art papers. They're somewhat stiff and hold a sharp crease when folded. The *Book-Stitched Bracelet* (page 102) is a perfect example of incorporating that sharp fold into the design of project, while the *Vellum & Pearl Earrings* (page 53) use the stiffness of the paper to make a graceful paper curve. The translucent quality of vellum is an integral part of the design for the *Ethereal Leaf Earrings* (page 90). When you glue these papers, avoid using broad strokes of glue. Instead, apply tiny dots to prevent disfiguring glue stains and wrinkling.

PRINTED PAPERS

Gift-wrap papers, both coated and uncoated, are available in flat or folded sheets, as well as rolled lengths. Machine-printed patterns imitate calligraphy, intricate fabric patterns, and hand-blocked patterns. Papers sold for scrapbook or memory album crafting are available in a mind-boggling profusion of patterns, finishes, and textures. Japanese washi papers are printed with intricate patterns on fine-grained paper, and they're great to work with. Other handmade Asian papers often are decorated with clean-lined stenciled patterns or hand-printed patterns from hand-carved wood blocks.

HANDMADE PAPERS

The textures and patterns of handmade papers are seductive. Mulberry paper, made from the bark of the mulberry tree, is one of the original handmade art papers. It has the distinctive quality of producing nicely feathered edges, gorgeous colors, and interesting textures, as seen in the *Mulberry Bangles* (page 122) and the *Nature-In-Paper Brooches* (page 84). The strong, exquisite fibers of lokta paper, made in the Himalayan Mountain region of Nepal, make it an excellent choice for the *Accordion Pendant* (page 116). Handmade paper enthusiasts prize sheets of papers with names like *unryu*, *sunomi*, *hosho*, and *momiji*. Solid sheets formed with long, visible fibers and natural inclusions or sheets as delicate as handmade lace are just a few varieties. Crisp sheets, thick, textured sheets, and even rolls of fabric-like paper are a delight to the eye and touch.

POLYETHYLENE FIBER

Artists are known to look at every material and object for its possible use in their work. So it is with high-density polyethylene fiber, a material that we now see and touch almost daily. The product is frequently used for envelopes and other packaging for mailing and shipping, as well as for protective apparel, signs and banners, and even energy-saving house wrap.

The spun-bonded polyethylene also makes an innovative material for handcrafting, combining some of the properties of paper, cloth, and film. It is bright-white, strong, lightweight, flexible, and silky smooth, as well as resistant to water, abrasion, and aging. It can be cut, glued, and nicely colored with dyes or permanent markers. The *Interlocking Necklace & Bracelets* (page 80) are constructed using this versatile product.

TOOLS & SUPPLIES FOR PAPER

Many of the tools and supplies needed for crafting paper you'll be familiar with and may already have on hand. Don't feel that you have to run out and purchase a specific item (unless, of course, you really feel you have to have one). Use your common sense and ingenuity to improvise when needed.

HANDY TOOLS

Metal-edge rulers are indispensable. The metal edge ensures straight and accurate edges as you cut against them with sharp craft knives. You can also tear paper against the edge of the ruler to create a straight, softly torn appearance.

A bone folder is an excellent tool for creasing and scoring paper. In a pinch, the dull blade of a table knife is an acceptable substitute.

Good quality drawing pencils and a small pencil sharpener should be in your toolbox. A sharpened pencil marks a fine, well-defined line for cutting. Lightly penciled registration marks make it easy for you to place cut-paper motifs accurately on flat surfaces. A soft, kneaded eraser is also nice to have.

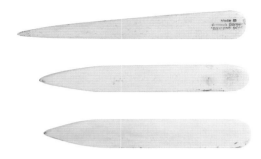

BONE FOLDERS

A French curve and a compass are great for drawing fluid curved lines or creating circular shapes. You can also use plates, drinking glasses, or saucers as templates to mark curves or circles.

Technically speaking, waxed paper is a material, but it's a useful tool as well. Use a sheet of waxed paper to protect glued surfaces when you press them with a weight. Glued surfaces dry with less wrinkling when weighted, so put your old textbooks or dictionary to good use as pressing tools.

Keep a selection of paintbrushes at hand for gluing, painting, and varnishing paper. A well-made glue brush with soft bristles is a wise investment. The flexible bristles make coating paper with an even coat of glue a snap. Take care of your brush and clean it in warm, soapy water after each and every use. Stencil brushes and other paintbrushes are valuable when working with paper.

FROM LEFT: METAL-EDGE RULER, CRAFT KNIFE

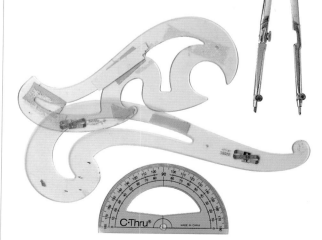

CLOCKWISE FROM LEFT: FRENCH CURVES, COMPASS, PROTRACTOR

Disposable latex gloves provide protection for your hands when you work with papier-mâché; unless you enjoy peeling a layer of dried glue from your fingers, you'll be wise to wear them.

Recycled materials such as food trays and plastic lids are excellent containers for glues, paints, and varnishes. Keep some on hand for a variety of crafting chores.

Pieces of soft cloth are also useful; use them to clean fingertips stained with glue and to wipe away excess glue from paper surfaces.

TAPES

Masking tapes in a variety of widths, types, and colors can always be put to good use. Black masking tape (purchased from an art supply store) has excellent adhesive qualities, in addition to having decorative potential. Low-tack painting tapes, because they are less likely to mar paper surfaces, are a good choice when you wish to hold papers together temporarily. Good quality white artists' tape is also convenient. Narrow, white drafting tape holds paper well and is not likely to mar paper surfaces. Use gummed paper tapes when constructing the basic structures for papier-mâché. Double-sided foam mounting tapes can be used to give layered papers dimension. Cellophane tapes, single and double-face, come in handy, too.

FROM LEFT: ACRYLIC MEDIUM, SPRAY ADHESIVE, DECOUPAGE MEDIUM, GLUE STICK, CELLOPHANE TAPE, MASKING TAPES, PAINTER'S TAPE

LESLIE MATTHEWS
Rock, Paper, Scissors, 2001
Largest pendant, 9 x 5 x 3.5 cm
Paper, color photocopies on tracing paper, steel cable, sterling silver; laminated, folded, glued
PHOTO © GRANT HANCOCK

HYESEUNG SHIN
Untitled, 2004
Ring, 4 x 5 x 2 cm; necklace, 45 x 10 x 2 cm
Wrapping paper, sterling silver
PHOTO © MOONK

DAYNA M. ORIONE-KIM
Lovers: Ohia and Lehua (Wedding Earpiece), 2004
13.3 x 11.4 x 5.1 cm
Handmade paper, sterling silver; sewn, soldered, hand fabricated
PHOTO © ALAN FARKAS

GLUES

Polyvinyl acetate (PVA) is one of the best glues to use with paper. It dries clear, and quickly, and is relatively inexpensive. Simple white craft glue is a PVA glue, and the terms can be used interchangeably. You can dilute the glue with water to make it more spreadable or to use for papiermâché. Other glues, such as wallpaper paste and rice-based glues, can be used as well.

Rubber cement is good when you need a temporary bond. A single coat of cement is repositionable. A more permanent bond can be created by coating both surfaces to be joined, letting the cement dry, and then pressing the surfaces together. Spray adhesives work in much the same way. They're handy when you have large surface areas to bond. Be sure to cover your work area to protect it from overspray, and work in a well-ventilated room when you use spray adhesives.

Semisolid glue sticks, epoxy glues, and hot glue can be used with paper, too. You can use a hot glue gun and glue sticks to join together and construct dimensional shapes from cardboard or foam-core board. Don't attempt to use hot glue as you would PVA glue. You won't be happy with the results. Decoupage mediums, acrylic varnishes, and acrylic mediums can also be used to adhere papers. They are available in matte, satin, and gloss finishes.

CUTTING TOOLS

A utility knife with breakaway blades is an ideal tool for cutting heavy cardboard. Craft knives with disposable blades are a must-have when you work with papers and lightweight board. Change the blades frequently: A dull blade will leave a ragged edge when you try to cut with it.

Keep your favorite pair of scissors close at hand when you work with paper. Handle scissors with sharp, curved blades and fine points with care. If they are treated like fine tools, their cost will be repaid over the years. There are many inexpensive scissors used for cutting decorative edges:

FROM LEFT: DECORATIVE-EDGE SCISSORS, ROTARY CUTTER, SEWING SCISSORS, SCISSORS

wavy, deckled, or geometric. Pinking shears are well-made sewing scissors that create decorative edges. Rotary cutters are packaged with circular blades made to cut straight-edged lines. They are useful when you need to make long, straight cuts. Manufacturers have created deckled and wavy-edged blades for rotary cutters.

A self-healing cutting mat is a necessity when using a craft knife, utility knife, or rotary cutter. If you don't have a self-healing mat, protect your work surface with a sheet of double-face cardboard or a thick magazine.

A paper cutter with a guillotine blade is great when you have to cut multiple sheets or many same-size pieces. You can find this type of cutter in a variety of sizes, from small personal models to the heavy-duty cutters found in copy shops and offices.

A circle cutter makes the challenge of cutting circles with perfect diameters and edges a snap. The tools come in a variety of sizes and options, so be sure to consider your particular needs before buying one. You'll find a circle cutter a handy tool for making the *Book-Stitched Bracelet* (page 102) and the *Noir Choker* (page 34), both using dozens of perfect circles in their construction.

CIRCLE CUTTER

PIERCING TOOLS

Manufacturers have created inexpensive hand punches that can pierce holes in a variety of sizes and shapes. Eyelet punches make holes into which decorative and functional eyelets can be set. The throat depth of the punch is the only limitation for its use. A hole punch must be used around the edges of a sheet of paper. If you need a hole in the center of a sheet of paper much wider than 2 inches (5.1 cm), you'll need to cut it out with a sharp craft knife or scissors.

FROM LEFT: EYELET PLIERS, HOLE PUNCH, HAND PUNCH

TECHNIQUES FOR PAPER

DECOUPAGE

Decoupage, from the French verb *découper*, meaning "to cut out," is the technique of cutting and pasting paper to a surface to create an image or pattern. Just about any type of surface can be used for decoupage: metal, glass, wood, cloth, and paper, too.

Simply adhere cut paper shapes to a clean surface with PVA glue diluted with a little water or with commercially available decoupage mediums. Make sure the cut paper is laid smoothly on the surface without wrinkling or creating air bubbles. A sharp, straight pin is useful for puncturing air bubbles, which can then be smoothed into place with your fingers or a soft cloth. A final protective coat of acrylic varnish is brushed onto the entire surface to protect the applied papers.

FOLDING

One of the most useful properties of paper is that it can be folded to hold a sharp crease. On the other hand, a crease in paper is almost impossible to eliminate. That said, store your papers flat and be very sure you make a fold where you want it.

A single fold or crease will give a flat sheet just a hint of dimension. Combining multiple folds can create truly three-dimensional forms from a flat

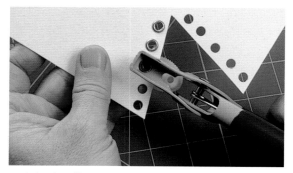

sheet. The Japanese art of origami is the most widely known technique for creating a three-dimensional form from a sheet of paper. Multiple folds can also be used to create simple forms that in turn can be joined to make sculptural shapes. Origami projects, such as the *Origami Crane Cocktail Ring* (page 126) and *Cut, Clarity, Color, Carat* (page 72) are examples of exceptional-al projects created just by folding paper.

STITCHING

Machine or hand stitching can be used to join sheets of paper much as you would fabric. Even

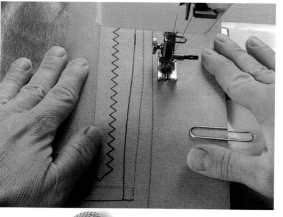

more exciting are the possi-bilities for using stitchery as a decorative element with paper. Experiment with the variety of stitches you can create by hand or with a machine. Stitching is used to join decorative papers for *Stuffed Pod Pendant* (page 98), and embroidery stitches are featured in the *Crimson Grid Brooch* (page 44).

CUTTING & PIERCING

You can make sharp, clean-edged straight cuts with scissors or a sharp knife drawn against a

metal ruler. If you want a softer edge, tear the paper against a metal ruler, or fold the paper and tear along the crease. Handmade papers with long fibers can be cut with scissors, but they look best when torn.

When you want to cut out printed or traced shapes, first cut out the unwanted internal sec-tions with a craft knife or sharp, pointed scissors. Then cut out the external edge of the shape. You'll find that you can make a smoother cut by moving the paper towards the scissor blades rather than pushing the scissors forward. You can pierce paper with a variety of punches, needles, or awls. Holes can be functional or decorative, as shown in the photo above.

PAPIER-MÂCHÉ

Papier-mâché is the craft of modeling three-dimensional shapes with pasted, torn paper strips. Papier-mâché projects are often constructed with double-wall cardboard bases. The bases always should be coated with lightly diluted PVA glue and allowed to dry. This seals the cardboard and pre-vents it from absorbing excessive amounts of moisture during construction. Other bases should

be coated with a thin layer of petroleum jelly before the papier-mâché mixture is applied to them.

Be sure to try the instant papier-mâché products now available in retail stores. Mixed with water, this relatively new material handles like clay but needs no firing. Dried forms can be sawed, sanded, nailed, waterproofed, and painted, providing a broad range of creative design, such as for the *Take Six Necklace* (page 42).

Papier-mâché is a gleefully messy business—there's no getting around it (see lower right photo, page 14). Cover your work area with plastic sheeting or plastic trash bags. Wear a pair of disposable latex gloves, unless you don't mind tediously scrubbing your hands and peeling off layers of dried PVA glue.

LAMINATING

Lamination sandwiches paper between two layers of plastic film. The laminate film protects paper from moisture, oil, dirt, grease, and wear. Lamination film is available in both gloss and matte finishes and is applied using either a hot or cold process.

Heat-sealed laminating film is usually found in commercial and school applications. Office supply stores carry heat-laminating systems or dry-mounting presses for small business use. Most copy shops provide inexpensive laminating services. Heat-sealed laminating films are usually thicker and more durable than cold-laminating films.

Cold-laminating film—clear adhesive shelf paper is one common type—requires no heat to seal the paper between the layers. There are several brands of clear adhesive papers available. Craft stores usually carry one or more brands of clear adhesive papers and cold lamination systems as well. The cold lamination systems sold in craft stores are easy to use at home. Several of these machines offer additional features, such as applying adhesives to paper items. The laminating process is described and used artistically in the *Golden Paper Crystals* (page 38) and the *Blooming Charm Bracelet* (page 56).

CAROL WINDSOR
Orange Heart Leaf Necklace, 2002
90 x 5 x 2 cm
Sterling silver, mulberry, Japanese, and Nepalese papers; oxidized, hand fabricated, laminated
PHOTO © GEORGE POST

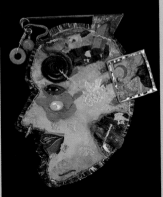

KEN BOVA
Tuff, 2000
9 x 7.5 x 1 cm
Sterling silver, 23-karat gold leaf, rag paper, French currency, postcard, quartz, apatite, pearl, glass, acrylic, pastel
PHOTO © ARTIST

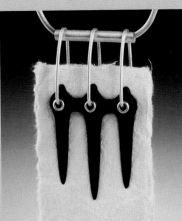

CODY BUSH
Untitled, 2005
13 x 6.5 x 2 cm
Handmade paper, sterling silver, aluminum; digitally milled, anodized, soldered, riveted
PHOTO © ARTIST

METAL

Most jewelry, even paper jewelry, usually includes metals. Following are some properties and characteristics of the most common types.

SILVER

A beautiful and durable material, sterling silver is basically the standard silver used in jewelry today. Contrary to popular belief, sterling silver isn't pure silver. Pure silver, commonly called fine silver, is a fairly soft metal. To boost pure silver's strength, it's combined with an alloy. The most common metal with which silver is combined is copper. The composition of sterling silver is 92.5 percent silver and 7.5 percent copper.

GOLD

Like pure silver, pure gold is much too soft, and therefore impractical, for most jewelry making, so it's usually mixed with other metals to make it more stable and more versatile. The measuring scale in the United States for indicating the purity of gold is the karat, and the higher the percentage of pure gold the higher the karat. Metals that are mixed with pure gold for strength can also change the color of the gold, resulting in different shades of yellow, white, pink, and even green gold.

COPPER

Copper is a pure metal that is initially bright reddish brown in color. Copper can also acquire rich green and brick red patinas through chemical or heat treatments. Copper is highly malleable, making it easy to work, and low in cost, making it a popular metal, especially for beginning jewelers.

OTHER METALS

Naturally good-looking, with a highly reflective grayish white color, aluminum is also lightweight (about one third as heavy as copper or steel). Soft and malleable, aluminum is extremely easy to form, machine, and cast. Brass is an alloy of copper and zinc that has been used and prized since ancient times for its golden hue, hardness, and workability. Steel is the common name for a large family of iron alloys commonly made from iron ore, coal, and limestone. There are currently more than 3,500 different grades of steel with many different physical and chemical properties. Stainless steel is a broad term for a group of corrosion-resistant steels that contain chromium. There are many other interesting metals with which you can experiment, such as bronze, nickel silver, niobium, pewter, and titanium.

METAL FORMS

Most of the metal forms you'll need are readily available from jewelry, bead, and metal suppliers. I encourage you to order a catalog from one or more sources and browse their enormous selection.

ASSORTED BASE METAL WIRES

■ SHEET METAL

Flat sheets of both precious and base metals are manufactured and sold in different sizes. The thickness of the metal is referred to as its gauge. Gauge numbers inversely specify the thickness of the metal—the thinner the metal, the higher its gauge number. In addition to the ordinary square and rectangular sheets, metal suppliers also sell many precut flat shapes such as circles and triangles, and even more intricate designs, such as stars, leaves, and animals.

■ WIRE, ROD & TUBING

Metal wire is manufactured with many different profiles and in many different thicknesses. Round wire is the most common shape, but there is also half round, square, triangular, and more. Like sheet metal, the thickness of wire is measured using the gauge system. Precious metal wires are cut to the length ordered and priced by weight. Because they are less expensive, base metal wires are generally sold in predetermined lengths on a spool or in a coil. Metal rod is measured incrementally in millimeters rather than gauge and is available in larger sizes. Tubing is a hollow metal cylinder. It's manufactured and sold with different wall thicknesses and diameters. Both of these measurements are given in millimeters rather than gauge. A tube has two diameters. One is measured outside the tube wall (the outside diameter, or *OD*), and one is measured inside the tube wall (the inside diameter, or *ID*).

GALLERY

TOOLS & SUPPLIES FOR METAL

You don't need to run out and buy a bunch of new tools to begin adding metal to your paper jewelry projects. Here is a survey of the most common tools and supplies used for metalwork. Gradually purchase them as needed.

JEWELER'S BENCH & BENCH PIN

A jeweler's bench is a wooden workstation specifically designed to meet the needs of metalsmiths. It has such features as tool drawers, catch trays, and precut holes to hold bench pins and mandrels. (A standard wooden bench pin is used to support metal for sawing, filing, etc. Most pins have a V-shaped slot cut in at least one side.) Because a jeweler's bench is a well-crafted piece of furniture, it is a major investment. However, a sturdy wooden table with an attachable clamp to hold a bench pin is a perfectly acceptable setup if you're just starting out.

SCRIBE

A scribe is a pointed tool used to make marks on metal. You'll use a scribe to draw points and lines or to transfer designs. Make your own scribe by sharpening the end of a piece of scrap metal (such as a nail), or you can purchase a commercial scribe.

STAINLESS STEEL RULER

The precision and durability of a short stainless steel ruler is invaluable to any jeweler. This compact measuring device is easy to maneuver on small surfaces and resists damage well. Its lengths are given in small, easily divisible metric increments, such as centimeters and millimeters.

SEPARATORS, CALIPERS & TEMPLATES

Separators make measuring equal distances simple and precise. Simply set the two metal arms apart at the desired space, lock in this length, and measure the metal. Calipers are used chiefly to measure thickness (gauge) or diameter. Each pair usually has two adjustable jaws. Use calipers to measure sheet metal, wire, rod, or tubing gauge. Having a selection of design templates is helpful for scribing common shapes onto metal. The templates can be plastic or metal with various sizes of cut-out circles, ovals, squares, triangles, and more.

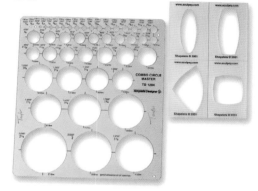

SHEARS, SNIPS & CLIPPERS

With handheld metal shears, you can cut straight or curved lines in metal sheet. Shears with smaller blades allow you to cut more intricate contours and patterns. Larger, table-mounted shears are also available. Snips, also known as cutters, are made for cutting wire. They have either flush or angled blades. Large-size nail clippers are also handy for cutting some types of wire.

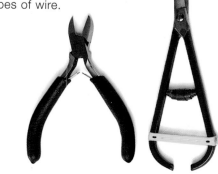

SAW FRAME & SAW BLADES

A high-quality, well-balanced jeweler's saw is one of the most important tools you can buy for metalworking. The open frame is made of rigid steel and can be adjusted for blade length and tension. The saw grip should be comfortable to hold. The throat depth of a jeweler's saw is the distance from the blade to the opposite vertical frame element. On standard frames, the throat depth ranges from 2¼ to 6 inches (5.7 to 15.2 cm).

Saw blades are made from steel and steel alloys, and are manufactured in different sizes: 1/0, 2/0, and 3/0 are the most popular. Each brand of blade has a different thickness, depth, and teeth per 1 inch (2.5 cm). Good saw blades have straight, uniform teeth and are flexible. Though they are more expensive, high-quality saw blades resist breakage and last longer, usually until they become dull.

METAL FILES

Use metal files to smooth the edge of sawed sheet metal, wire, or tubing. They are constructed from a strong, tool-steel alloy and, with proper care, they should last a long time. The broad term that describes all manual files used to remove, shape, or finish metal is hand file. These are generally 8 inches (20.3 cm) in total length with a cutting distance of 6 inches (15.2 cm). A hand file's "cut" size can range from very coarse to very fine. Hand files also come with many different profiles: the most popular are flat, barrette, half round, and square. Needle files are shorter, usually only 6 inches (15.2 cm) in total length, and much more narrow than hand files. They have a fine cut that

is perfect for finishing and smoothing small metal elements, and their thin shape makes it easy to reach into tight areas.

CHASING HAMMER

Specifically designed and weighted for metalworking, the head of a chasing hammer is made of polished steel and has two faces with different shapes. One face is wide, smooth, and slightly convex. The opposite end is ball-shaped.

FROM TOP:
CHASING HAMMER,
MALLET

MALLETS

Wooden, rawhide, or rubber mallets are exceptional tools for forming, bending, and flattening metal. Large hammers with wide cylindrical heads and two flat faces, their greatest advantage is that they move metal without marring, scratching, or damaging its surface.

STEEL BLOCK

Whether you're working at a jeweler's bench or on a worktable, it's most effective to hammer and form metal on top of a rigid steel block. The best bench blocks are made from tool steel that has been ground flat and polished. Most blocks range from 2½ to 5 inches (6.4 cm to 12.7 cm) square.

STEEL BLOCK,
RING MANDREL,
BEZEL MANDREL

MANDRELS

A mandrel is any type of sturdy form around which you can shape, straighten, or size metal. Commercial ring, bracelet, and necklace mandrels are made of metal or wood. Ring mandrels are tapered and marked with standard ring sizes. Bracelet mandrels have a gradual taper without markings, and necklace mandrels are designed to show how a piece will drape on the neck. You can hammer metal directly on or around most commercial mandrels. Feel free to use any common household item as a mandrel. Dowels and rods, even pencils, knitting needles, chopsticks, and rolling pins can be practical stand-ins.

PLIERS

Jeweler's pliers come in many different forms, most of them easily identifiable by a name that corresponds to their jaw shape. Round-nose pliers have fully rounded jaws that taper up from the base. Chain-nose pliers are round on the outside of the jaw but flat on the inside, tapering up to a point. Flat-nose pliers have flat and flush interior surfaces. The outside surfaces of their jaws are flat and angled. Round-nose, chain-nose, and flat-nose pliers are commonly made of stainless steel or tool steel and are available in short and long jaw lengths. Although these three types of pliers will handle most jobs, there are many other specialty pliers that are worth investigating.

CENTER PUNCH

A center punch is a tool with one pointed end used to make a small dent on a metal surface prior to drilling. Standard center punches have one flat end that must be tapped with a hammer to make an indention. Automatic punches have an adjustable internal hammer that releases when the punch is pressed down on the metal (see photo). You can use a nail as a center punch if you sharpen its tip.

FLEXIBLE SHAFT MACHINE

A flexible shaft machine is the jeweler's equivalent of a drill. It consists of a motor and a hand piece to which many devices, such as drill bits, burrs, cutters, and sanding disks, can be attached.
Most flexible shaft machines are run by foot pedals, allowing you to control the speed of the motor. A long flexible shaft connects the motor to the hand piece.

DRILL BITS

Metal drill bits for jewelry making are much smaller than average drill bits. The chuck in the flexible shaft machine is specially sized to accommodate these smaller attachments. Most bits are made from hard, polished steel and can sustain the high speeds of the flexible shaft machine. Most bits are measured by their diameter in millimeters, but some are manufactured and labeled to correspond with wire gauge sizes.

FLARING TOOL

A flaring tool stretches open, or flares, the ends of tube rivets. These metal tools are available commercially or can be hand made from any number of materials as long as one end is tapered and one is flat for hammering. A worn-out flexible shaft attachment or an old chasing tool makes a fine flaring tool.

BURNISHER

A burnisher is a versatile metalworking hand tool. Use it to gently shape and smooth metals, to open or close bezel settings, to even out surface imperfections, and to polish hard-to-reach places. Standard burnishers have wooden handles for a comfortable grip. The opposite, working, end may be straight or bent.

ADHESIVES

If you want to use an adhesive to join jewelry components, choose one that bonds quickly and stays strong. A colorless adhesive is generally preferable. Two-part epoxy (below, right) comes in two vials or syringes, the contents of which combine to form a very strong bond. Epoxies work well on a wide variety of materials, including metal, plastic, rubber, leather, stone, glass, and ceramics. Follow the manufacturer's directions to

mix the specific proportions of the two parts together, stirring it with a wooden tongue depressor, and applying it quickly. Use epoxies in a well-ventilated area and avoid breathing the fumes. Cyanoacrylate glues bond similar and dissimilar materials instantly—including your skin—so use them with care.

SANDING PAPERS & SCRUBBERS

Abrasive papers used to sand metal are made differently from those for sanding wood. Their grit is attached to the paper with a stronger fixative. This bond allows the abrasive to effectively shape and finish the metal, and it gives the paper a longer working life and the ability to be used both wet and dry. Metal sanding papers come in many grit sizes from coarse to fine. Higher numbered papers have finer grits. Most jewelers prefer 220-, 400-, and 600-grit papers. Green kitchen scrub pads and different grades of steel wool are also commonly used for sanding and finishing metal.

JEWELRY FINDINGS

Findings are components that ease the jewelry-making process or make finished pieces wearable. Jewelry and beading supply stores and catalogs sell an incredible variety of mass-produced findings for those who do not wish to make their own. Commercial findings come in lots of different metal types, including gold, gold-filled, sterling silver, brass, and surgical steel. Common findings include bead and end caps, crimp beads, jump rings, head and eye pins, bales, clasps, pin backs, ear wires, ear posts, and nuts.

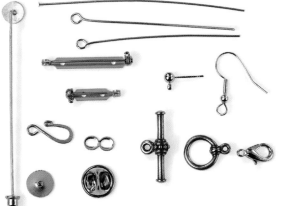

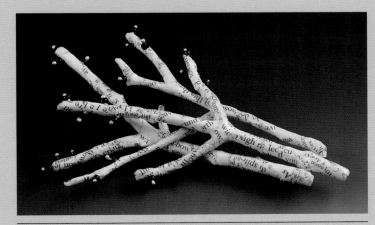

ANDREA SHAVLIK
Twig Brooch, 2006
13 x 8 x 2 cm
Book pages, sterling silver, seed beads; collaged
PHOTO © YUKO YAGISAWA

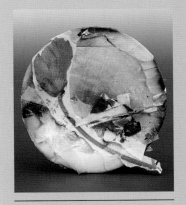

ANGELA ZENT
Untitled, 2006
6 x 6 x 0.5 cm
Shell, gum wrapper, wax paper bag, paper towel, copper, tape, masking tape, safety pin, nail lacquer; hand fabricated, burned
PHOTO © JEFFREY SABO

SHIM SU HYUN
Nature II, 2005
140 x 7 x 5 cm
Paper
PHOTO © IN SOO LEE

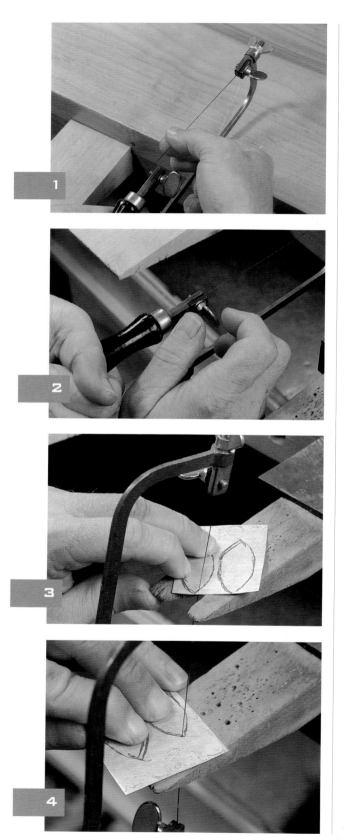

METALWORKING TECHNIQUES

Basic metalworking skills include sawing, piercing, and riveting. Read through the different procedures carefully, and then give them a trial run. They will become easier with practice. When making the projects later in the book, refer to this section to refresh your knowledge as needed.

SAWING METAL

To saw metal, you'll need a jeweler's saw and saw blades, a bench pin, and sheet metal. If you're new to this process, I recommend practicing on scrap sheet.

■ INSTALLING A SAW BLADE INTO A SAW FRAME

1. Open the saw frame's jaw approximately 10 mm shorter than the length of the blade. Insert the blade into the top nut of the frame, with the teeth facing away from the neck and pointing down. Tighten the nut (photo 1).

2. Rest the end of the saw frame handle on your sternum, and rest the top edge of the saw frame against the edge of a worktable or jeweler's bench. Use your sternum to press the saw handle and slightly shorten the length of the jaw.

3. Place the free end of the saw blade into the lower nut and tighten (photo 2). Release the pressure on the saw handle. The blade should be stretched tight in the frame.

■ SAWING STEPS

1. Hold the saw in your hand lightly. The temptation to press too hard is great, and most beginning metalworkers break a lot of saw blades by exerting excess pressure.

2. Place the metal on the bench pin. Position the saw blade at a 90-degree angle to the metal. Move the saw frame up and down, keeping the frame pointing forward (photo 3). The teeth of the blade will cut the metal only on the downward stroke.

Note: Turn the metal, not the saw frame, when making a rounded cut. To make a tight rounded cut, simultaneously turn the metal and the saw while quickly moving the frame up and down (photo 4).

DRILLING & PIERCING METAL

Drilling and piercing metal is a three-step process. It consists of drilling a hole, feeding a saw blade through the hole, then sawing a shape in the surface of the sheet.

MATERIALS

Sheet metal

TOOLBOX

Steel block

Center punch

Chasing hammer

Small drill bit

Flexible shaft machine

Scrap block of wood

Jeweler's saw and saw blades

STEP BY STEP

1. Place the sheet metal on the steel block. Position the center punch at the point where you want to drill the hole (photo 5). Use the hammer to lightly strike the top of the center punch, creating a dimple or small indentation on the metal.

2. Insert a drill bit into the flexible shaft machine. Place the dimpled sheet metal on the wood block and drill the hole (photo 6).

3. Detach the bottom end of the saw blade from the frame. Thread this end through the drilled hole. Reattach the blade to the frame. Saw the metal to cut out the interior shape (photo 7).

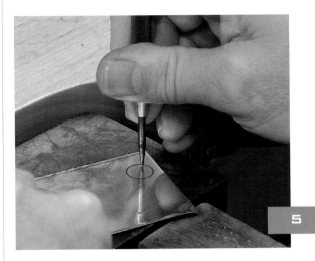

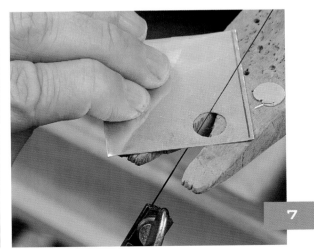

FILING METAL

All sawed metal pieces have sharp edges that should be removed with a file for safe handling. Metal can also be shaped and contoured with a file. The teeth on the file are angled away from the handle. This means that all cutting is accomplished on the file's forward stroke. Any pressure applied on the back stroke only wears down the file.

1. Secure the metal to be filed against a work-table or bench. Select the coarsest file needed to begin taking away the metal.

2. Place your index finger on the top of the file. Press down as you slide the file forward against the metal. Lift the file off the metal as you bring it back and reposition it for another stroke (photo 8).

3. Repeat steps 1 and 2 with a sequence of finer files to complete the process.

FORMING METAL

To form sheet metal is to coax it into a dimensional shape. There are many techniques you can use to accomplish this. Bending by hand is perhaps the most simple. Other options include hammering sheet around a mandrel (photo 9) or into a depression, using a dapping block and dap (photo 10), forging, and using a die press. When metal is formed, especially with a hammer, its molecular structure changes. The longer it's worked, the harder and more brittle it becomes. This change is called work hardening, and it can be reversed through the process of annealing.

MAKING COLD CONNECTIONS

Paper and metal elements can be joined in many ways without soldering. These methods are called cold-connection techniques and include riveting, using jump rings, wire wrapping, sewing, and adhesives.

RIVETING

A rivet is a piece of wire or tube fed through a hole and flared on each end to hold two pieces of metal together.

▪ MAKING A WIRE OR TUBE RIVET

MATERIALS

Sheet metal to be joined

Wire or tubing for rivet

TOOLBOX

Calipers (preferred) or metal ruler

Jeweler's saw and saw blades

Wet/dry sandpaper

Drill bit, same diameter as wire or tube rivet

Steel block

Center punch

Chasing hammer

Flexible shaft machine or small motorized rotary tool

Flaring tool (for tube rivets only)

STEP BY STEP

1. Use calipers or a ruler to measure the combined thickness of the metals to be joined (photo 11). Add approximately ³⁄₃₂ inch (2 mm) to this measurement.

2. Use the jeweler's saw to cut a corresponding length of wire or tube. Sand the ends of the cut wire or tube.

11

GALLERY

ANIKA SMULOVITZ
Love Token (Engagement Rings #1–5)
from the *Chocolate Series*, 2002
Each, 5.4 x 4.4 x 4.4 cm
Chocolate boxes, chocolate wrappers;
scored, folded, glued
PHOTO © ARTIST

MARY HALLAM PEARSE
Residue Brooch, 2005
3 x 2.7 x 1.5 cm
Paper, sterling silver; cast
PHOTO © ARTIST

CAROL WINDSOR
*Purple Blossom
Necklace*, 2003
5.5 x 45 x 2.5 cm
Paper, sterling silver,
amethyst, pearls, fixative;
oxidized, laminated,
textured, bent, ground
PHOTO © GEORGE POST

3. Using a bit that is the same diameter as the wire or tube, drill a hole through each metal piece at the point they are to be riveted (photo 12). (Refer to page 23 for basic drilling instructions.) Thread the wire or tube through the drilled holes and place the metal on top of a steel block.

4. For wire riveting: gently tap one end of the wire two or three times with a chasing hammer (photo 13). Turn over the metal piece and adjust the wire so there is an equal length sticking out of each side of the hole. Gently tap two or three times on the reverse side. Repeat this process— tapping, turning, and adjusting—until the wire ends flare, forming the rivet and making a secure connection.

For tube riveting: insert a flaring tool into one end of the tubing. Use a chasing hammer to make one light tap on the flaring tool (photo 14). Turn over the metal piece, insert the flaring tool into the opposite tubing end, and make another light tap. Repeat this process, adjusting the tube so an equal length sticks out of each side of the hole, and make one tap on each tubing end until the tubing cannot be removed from the hole. At this point, tap gently and directly on the tubing with the ball side of the chasing hammer (photo 15). Repeatedly turn the metal over in order to tap an equal amount on both sides until the rivet is secure.

JUMP RINGS

Wire circles, known as jump rings, are a simple way to hold jewelry components together, becoming a part of the jewelry design at the same time, such as in the *Blooming Charm Bracelet* (page 56). For the *Knitted Paper Necklace* (page 108), shiny copper jump rings provide contrasts of color and texture in addition to their functional role.

The rings are split so they can be opened and closed with pliers. Although jump rings are commercially available, you can easily make them yourself from almost any gauge wire.

■ MAKING JUMP RINGS

MATERIALS

Wire, gauge of your choice

TOOLBOX

Mandrel, diameter equal to the size jump rings you wish to make

Wire snips

Jeweler's saw and saw blades

Pliers

STEP BY STEP

1. Cut a piece of wire and coil it tightly around the mandrel (photo 16). (Each full wrap makes one jump ring.) Slide the wire coil off the mandrel. If the coil is longer than 1 or 1½ inches (2.5 or 3.8 cm), trim it down so it will be easier to hold and saw.

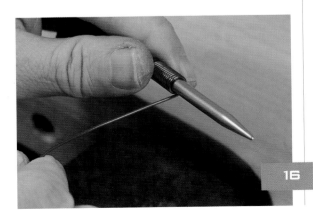

16

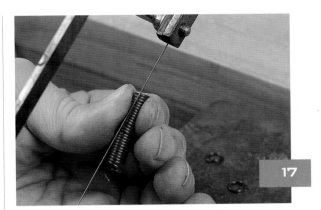

17

2. Hold the coil in your fingers on top of the bench pin. Use your other hand to hold the jeweler's saw at a slight angle. Carefully saw down the length of the coil (photo 17).

■ USING JUMP RINGS

■ To open and close a jump ring, move its ends from side to side on the same plane.

■ Only open a jump ring as much as is needed to insert the objects being joined; otherwise, the ring's shape can become distorted.

PLASTICS

Using plastics, such as acrylic and laminates, is an innovative and easy way to inject a dose of color and transparency into paper jewelry.

ACRYLIC SHEET

Acrylic is available in clear, transparent, or opaque sheets and in precut shapes. The *Mulberry Bangles* (page 122) and the *Art of Geometry Brooch* (page 68) both use acrylic sheets to provide the structure for these pieces of imaginative jewelry. When working with acrylic sheet or shapes, always leave the paper masking film on as long as possible. Except for intricate detail work, you should remove the masking only when your project is completed.

If you purchase acrylic sheet from your local glass shop or home improvement store, have them cut it to size or close to the size you need. Then use a jeweler's saw to cut the acrylic to the exact size or shape you need (photo 18). If you need to cut a sheet at home, follow the method described below.

■ SCORING & BREAKING ACRYLIC SHEET

A method similar to that used to cut glass is used to cut acrylic sheet up to 3/16 inch (5 mm) thick.

MATERIALS

Acrylic sheet

TOOLBOX

Straightedge

Scribe, awl, or utility knife

Clamp (optional)

STEP BY STEP

1. Place a straightedge on the sheet and hold it firmly in place.

2. Score the sheet by drawing a scribe, an awl, or a utility knife along the edge of the straightedge several times (seven or eight times for a 3/16-inch [5 mm] sheet).

3. Clamp the sheet or firmly hold it under a straightedge with the scored mark hanging just over the edge of a table.

4. Apply a sharp downward pressure to break the sheet along the scored line.

■ DRILLING A HOLE IN ACRYLIC OR PLASTIC

If you can find them, use plastic-cutting bits for drilling these materials. If not, follow these suggestions for using conventional drill bits.

■ Use a slow to medium speed to drill plastics (photo 19). High speeds cause the material to melt.

■ As you drill, lift the bit to allow the debris to come to the surface.

■ Dip the drill bit into a small container of water as you work. Doing so prevents the bit from becoming too hot and melting the plastic.

■ FILING, SANDING & FINISHING ACRYLIC

Once you've sawn out an acrylic shape, use a smooth cut file to file its edges and remove tool marks. File only in one direction, then proceed to 120-grit sandpaper if needed. Use 220- and 400-grit wet/dry papers to finish the job. Wrapping the sandpaper around a sanding block will help you keep the edges of the acrylic perpendicular, and your fingers won't get as tired. Final polishing gives acrylic a high luster. Power-driven buffing tools are recommended. A handheld motorized tool with a buffing wheel attachment also works well for this type of job. To rub out a scratch, be sure to sand an area larger than the scratch. Use fine-grit wet/dry sandpapers in a circular motion with a light touch and plenty of water.

BEADING

A bead can be anything that has a hole through it. *Cherry Orb Necklace* (page 30) illustrates an inspired use of small foam shapes, each covered with bits of paper in a decoupage process, to make a piece of wearable art.

There are many, many materials on which to hang or string beads. Bead thread is a strong, thin thread that resists fraying. Usually synthetic, it is perfect for both stringing and sewing beads. Monofilaments, tigertail (a tiny version of steel cable), and decorative threads such as leather, linen, satin, or silk can all be used to string beads. And don't forget found or repurposed materials such as rubber cord, string, ball chain, and even industrial wire.

FROM TOP: COMMERCIAL BEADS IN DIFFERENT SHAPES, SIZES, AND COLORS; ASSORTED STRINGING CABLES AND THREADS

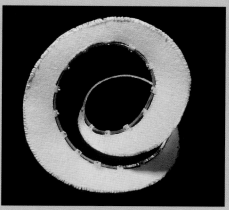

FABIANA GADANO
Viento Bracelet, 2003
15 x 14 x 9 cm
Rag paper, sterling silver, handmade paper; riveted
PHOTO © PATRICIO GATTI

KRISTI KLOSS
Luneria Brooch, 2005
11 x 7.5 x 0.5 cm
Sterling silver, scrapbooking paper, mother-of-pearl; hand fabricated, bezel set
PHOTO © KAREN CARTER
COURTESY OF SHERRIE GALLERIE, COLUMBUS, OHIO

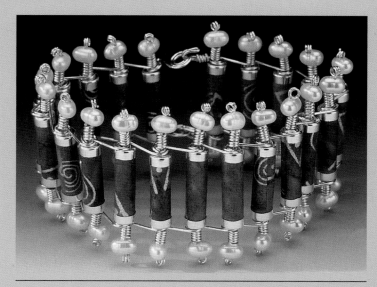

NICOLETTE TALLMADGE
Untitled, 2004
3.8 x 19.1 x 1 cm
Rolled cotton rag paper, sterling silver wire, freshwater pearls
PHOTO © JERRY ANTHONY

CHERRY ORB NECKLACE

RICH RED BEADS WITH DAZZLING GOLD ACCENTS MAKE THIS NECKLACE OPULENT. STRING YOUR COLLAGED CREATIONS ON MULTIPLE SILK BEADING CORDS TO COMPLETE THE LUXURIOUS LOOK.

MATERIALS

7 polystyrene foam shapes, precut spheres or beads or hand carved forms of your choice, each approximately 1 inch (2.5 cm) in diameter

Recycled paper of your choice, such as newspaper, stamps, wrapping paper, or origami paper

White craft glue

3 silk beading cords, each 43 inches (109.2 cm) long, colors of your choice

8 commercial accent beads of your choice

TOOLBOX

Large sewing needle

Container for glue and water mixture

Toothpicks

Tweezers

Ruler

STEP BY STEP

1. If needed, make a hole in each of the polystyrene foam shapes with a large sewing needle. (Some polystyrene beads are manufactured with holes.)

2. Tear the recycled paper into tiny pieces. Mix a solution of white craft glue and water that is three parts water to one part glue. Soak the torn paper pieces in the thin glue solution until they are soft.

3. Place one polystyrene bead on a toothpick. Use tweezers to pick up the small pieces of paper and place them on the bead. Let the bead dry for approximately 30 minutes. Use your finger to press the dry bead, making its surface smooth.

4. Cover the bead with a layer of the glue solution and let dry. Repeat this step at least five times.

5. Thread the three silk beading cords through the large sewing needle; then line up the ends of the cords and find their center. String one polystyrene bead onto the cords and push it down to the center point. Knot the cords on either side of the bead to prevent it from moving.

6. From the knot on one side of the polystyrene bead, measure 1½ to 1¾ inches (3.8 to 4.4 cm) and tie a knot in the three beading cords. String a commercial accent bead of your choice onto the cords and slide it down to the knot. Knot the cord on the other side of the bead. Measure 1½ to 1¾ inches (3.8 to 4.4 cm) from the last knot (after the commercial bead) and tie a knot in the three beading cords. String a polystyrene bead and tie a knot to secure it. Repeat this process, alternating beads, until three handmade beads and three commercial beads are strung up both sides of the center bead.

7. On one end of the necklace, measure 4 inches (10.2 cm) from the last knot and tie another knot in the cord. String a commercial bead and tie a knot on the loose end of the cord to secure it. Repeat this step on the opposite end of the necklace. To wear the necklace, tie a square knot just below the commercial beads at the two ends of the silk cord.

PEARLS & CARDBOARD CUFF

ELEGANT PEARLS, INFORMALLY SCATTERED AND SEWN ON ROUGH
PAPER, CREATE A BRACELET OF SURPRISING BEAUTY.

MATERIALS

Single-face cardboard (corrugated paper)*

Thread in color of your choice

Pearls, assorted diameters

TOOLBOX

Scissors or sharp craft knife

Sewing needle

*Use an old piece of cardboard that has been creased and crumpled, or rough one up to make it softer and more comfortable on the wrist.

STEP BY STEP

1. Use scissors or a sharp craft knife to cut out a rectangular piece of the single-face cardboard. The designer used a 3⅛ x 8⅝-inch (8 x 22 cm) rectangle, but feel free to alter these measurements based on how wide and how large you want the bracelet to be. Check the size by wrapping the piece of cardboard around your arm (or the arm of the person you're making it for), making sure the bracelet will be large enough to slip on and off when you stitch it together later.

2. Thread the sewing needle with the thread. (The designer selected a thread that matched the color of the pearls.) Sew the pearls onto the piece of corrugated cardboard so it looks like a pile of pearls has been scattered on the surface. Use your imagination—what would a scattered pile of pearls look like? The designer began by sewing a tight group of pearls in the middle of the card-board rectangle, and then gradually spread them out. She created contrast in the arrangement by including one pearl that is larger than the others.

3. Sew the ends of the bracelet together with the stitches of your choice. (A simple cross stitch was used on the featured project.)

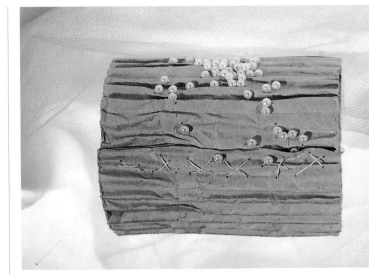

DESIGN IDEAS

■ Use very high-quality pearls to create more contrast between the inexpensive cardboard and the expensive pearls.

■ Substitute shimmering crystals or colorful seed beads for the pearls.

■ Disposable hot drink cup holders can also pro-vide a lovely background canvas for a scattered sea of pearls.

NOIR CHOKER

A FORMAL ARRANGEMENT OF 50 PAPER CIRCLES MAKES AN IMPRESSIVE VISUAL STATEMENT. VARY THE COLOR OF THE PAPER AND THE TYPE OF WIRE TO CREATE DIFFERENT STYLES.

MATERIALS

Cover stock paper, color of your choice

51 small silver beads, each 1.5 mm in diameter, hole at least 1 mm in diameter

Silver neck wire, 16 inches (40.6 cm) long

TOOLBOX

Cutting mat

Circle cutter

Straight pin

Chain-nose pliers

STEP BY STEP

1. Lay the cover stock paper on the cutting mat. Use the circle cutter to cut out 50 perfect paper circles, each with a ¾-inch (1.9 cm) diameter.

2. Use the straight pin to pierce a small hole in the center of each paper circle. If the hole is too large, the circles will not sit firmly on the neck wire.

3. Alternately thread a small silver bead and a paper circle onto the neck wire, continuing in this manner until you have strung all the circles. Center the paper circles and beads on the front of the neck wire.

4. Use the chain-nose pliers to gently crimp the last two silver beads onto the neck wire to prevent the paper circles from sliding apart.

TUBE & TISSUE BANGLE

DECOUPAGE CAN BE LIKE PAINTING WITH A PALETTE OF PAPER. LUSH JEWEL TONES AND INTERESTING TEXTURES MAKE THIS A STRIKING BRACELET.

MATERIALS

Double wall cardboard

Decoupage medium

Decorative tissue papers of your choice

TOOLBOX

Ruler

Craft knife

Paintbrush

Plastic yogurt container (optional)*

* Hint: When creating a circular bracelet, use a plastic yogurt container to maintain the bracelet's shape while the glue dries (figure 1).

STEP BY STEP

1. Determine the width and shape that you want for the bracelet, and then mark the corrugated cardboard to these measurements. (The designer's bangle bracelet is 2¼ inches [5.7 cm] tall with an outside diameter of 3¼ inches [8.3 cm]. The cardboard is ¼ inch [6 mm] thick.)

2. Using a craft knife, cut out the cardboard shape. If needed, bend the cardboard by scoring it along the corrugation (figure 2).

3. Use decoupage medium to adhere a thin layer of decorative tissue paper to all surfaces of the cardboard base. Let dry.

4. Adhere tissue paper accents on top of the base with decoupage medium. Create an artful design that appeals to you. Let dry.

5. To seal the bracelet, apply a thin and even coat of decoupage medium to its entire surface.

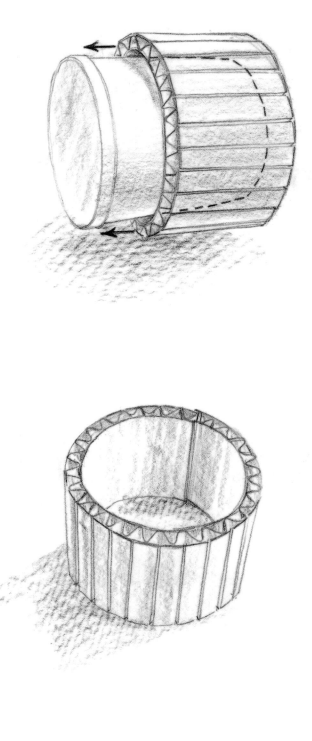

DESIGNER
JAMES BOVÉ AND
YOKO SEKINO-BOVÉ

GOLDEN PAPER CRYSTALS

A ADD A LITTLE SUNSHINE TO YOUR LIFE WITH THESE GORGEOUS
GEOMETRICAL BEADS. THIS DESIGN IS AN INGENIOUS WAY TO
PRESERVE PRINTED PAPERS YOU LOVE.

MATERIALS

Plain or decorative papers of your choice

Photocopied design template 1

Wire of your choice

Commercial neck wire or chain

TOOLBOX

Laminating machine (most print shops offer laminating services if you do not have a machine)

Permanent marker

Ruler

Scissors or craft knife

Pencil or scoring tool

Cyanoacrylate glue

Masking tape

Round-nose pliers

STEP BY STEP

1. Test a small sample of paper to make sure it can be laminated. Some papers are heat-sensitive, and they could melt in the machine. Laminate the paper you have selected and tested.

2. Trace the photocopied design template on the back of the laminated paper with a permanent marker. Trace one template for each bead you wish to make. (The designer created 10 crystal beads for this project.) The small tabs or strips on the edges of the shape help secure the folded bead.

3. Cut out the traced shape with scissors or a craft knife. Using a pencil or other tool, score the dotted folding lines to make the laminated paper easier to fold.

4. Bend and wrap one 3-inch (7.6 cm) length of metal wire for each paper cutout. Position the wire so that ½ inch (1.3 cm) extends past the edge of the paper.

5. Apply cyanoacrylate glue to the laminated paper shapes and wires and assemble the beads. Use a generous amount of glue at the top of the beads and at the seams. Hold each assembled piece for a few minutes, until the glue sets. Wrap all of the beads with masking tape and let dry overnight. Remove the masking tape.

6. Use round-nose pliers to bend the hanging wires into a loop (figure 2). Form the loop over a commercial neck wire or through links in a commercial chain. (The designer strung a series of hand rolled paper beads between each crystal form as unique spacing elements.)

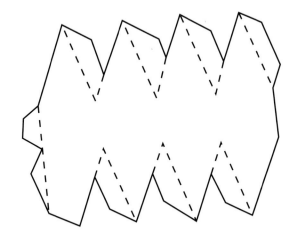

1

2

DAYBREAK BROOCH

DISPLAYING THE WARM COLORS OF A SCENIC SUNRISE, THIS STYLISH BROOCH BOASTS A MOST GRACEFUL COLLAGE. WELL-PLACED TOUCHES OF GOLD FOIL FURTHER ILLUMINATE THE COMPOSITION.

MATERIALS

Recycled magazines

Gold foil

Acrylic sheet, 2 x 2 x ³⁄₁₆ inch (5.1 x 5.1 x 0.5 cm)

Acrylic paint, black

Gel medium, matte

Acrylic spray varnish, gloss

Commercial pin back, self-adhesive

TOOLBOX

Plastic template, separators, or a compass

Jeweler's saw and saw blades

Sandpaper

Paintbrush

STEP BY STEP

1. Select, cut or tear out, and arrange colorful graphics from recycled magazines in a pleasing design. Judiciously work small pieces of gold foil into the design to strengthen its overall effect.

2. Use a plastic template, separators, or a compass to trace a circle with a 2-inch (5.1 cm) diameter onto the ³⁄₁₆-inch-thick (5 mm) acrylic sheet. Cut out the traced circle with a jeweler's saw.

3. Sand the edge, the top, and the bottom of the acrylic circle with sandpaper.

4. Use a paintbrush to apply black acrylic paint to the sanded acrylic circle. Paint all surfaces, including the edge, and let dry.

5. Use the matte gel medium to apply the paper and gold foil collage onto the painted acrylic circle. Let the gel medium dry completely.

6. Spray a thin and even layer of the acrylic spray varnish over the collage, and let dry. Add an additional coat if desired.

7. Attach the self-adhesive commercial pin back to the back of the collaged brooch.

DESIGN IDEA

■ With basic metalworking skills, you can bezel-set the collaged piece of acrylic. You can also attach handmade pin findings or scatter-pin clutches to the back of the bezel.

GALLERY

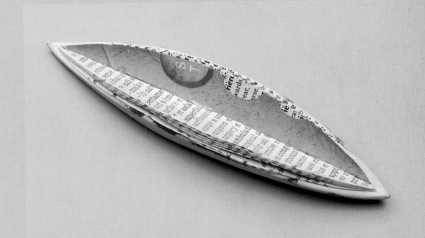

BOBBI GOODBOY
LOIS HARBAUGH
Red Text, 2005
10.7 x 2.2 x 2.2 cm
Cardboard, heavy paper, plaster, varnish, silver wire, dictionary pages, joss paper
PHOTO © TOM HOLT

DESIGNER
MARJORIE SCHICK

TAKE SIX NECKLACE

SCULPT BOLD BEADS IN ATTENTION-GRABBING SHAPES WITH INSTANT PAPIER-MÂCHÉ, AND THEN PAINT THE FORMS WITH VIBRANT COLORS TO COMPLETE THE DRAMATIC EFFECT.

MATERIALS

Instant papier-mâché

Waxed paper

Cellophane tape

Polystyrene foam or cardboard bases (optional)

White craft glue (optional)

Acrylic paints, in colors of your choice

Strong cord, such as nylon, to string the bead shapes

TOOLBOX

Bowl with a tight-fitting lid

Wood dowel, 4 inches (10.2 cm) long, diameter equal to the desired diameter for the hole in the beads

Sandpaper (optional)

Paintbrushes

STEP BY STEP

1. Mix the instant papier-mâché according to the manufacturer's instructions. Place the mixture in a bowl with a tight-fitting lid to keep it moist. The papier-mâché will be usable for several days if you keep it in a sealed container to prevent it from drying.

2. Wrap the dowel with waxed paper and tape the paper together on the ends. This way, you can pull the dowel out of one bead and use it for the next bead.

3. Sculpt the beads for the necklace, exploring both traditional and nontraditional shapes. The only requirement is that the beads have holes for stringing and that they fit against each other. If you want to make large beads, you can apply the papier-mâché over a polystyrene foam or cardboard base. Wet papier-mâché will also adhere to dry papier-mâché. (If in doubt, apply white craft glue to the completed form before adding new papier-mâché.)

4. Let the beads dry completely. Thick shapes will take several days.

5. The surface of the beads can be sanded, but the artist left these unfinished. Paint the beads with acrylic paints in any style you desire and let dry. Use any strong material to string the beads into a necklace. For this necklace, the artist used braided nylon blind cord that she purchased from a yacht store.

DESIGNER
FRANCINE HAYWOOD

CRIMSON GRID BROOCH

THE BRILLIANT DESIGN OF THIS BROOCH IS BOTH SEEN AND UNSEEN.
RED SILK CORD DELICATELY STITCHED ATOP WHITE PAPER IS CLEARLY
BEAUTIFUL, AND A CONCEALED PAIR OF RARE EARTH MAGNETS
INGENIOUSLY SECURES THE BROOCH TO A GARMENT.

MATERIALS

Heavy handmade paper or watercolor paper

Red silk beading cord, 0.018 inch (0.45 mm) in diameter

White craft glue

2 neodymium (rare earth) magnets

Two-part epoxy or other high-performance adhesive to glue magnet to paper

TOOLBOX

Ruler

Cutting mat

Scissors

Circle cutter (optional)

Square

Embroidery needle

MAKING A FRENCH KNOT STITCH

(Can be worked in any direction.)

Figure 1. Bring the needle up at point A. Hold the thread taut with the finger and thumb of your non-dominant hand. Tightly wind the thread once or twice (not more) around the needle tip.

Figure 2. Still holding the thread, insert the needle close to point A and pull it through to the back of the work, so the twists lie on the fabric surface neatly. Repeat as required.

STEP BY STEP

1. Measure and mark two circles on the heavy handmade or watercolor paper, one with a 2-inch (5.1 cm) diameter and one with a 1⅝-inch (4.1 cm) diameter. Carefully cut out both circles with scissors or the circle cutter.

2. On the back of the smaller paper circle, using the square as a guide, draw a centered ⁹⁄₁₆ x ⁹⁄₁₆-inch (12 x 12 mm) square. Measure and mark each side of the square at ³⁄₃₂-inch (2 mm) intervals and draw a grid (figure 3). Use a needle to pierce the points on the grid where the lines intersect, piercing a total of 49 holes.

3. Thread the red silk cord on a needle. Embroider one French knot for each pierced hole in the grid, twisting the thread twice around the needle on each stitch.

4. When the grid is filled with knots, bring the thread to the back of the paper circle. Securely knot the thread, and trim the end.

5. Place a dab of white craft glue in the middle of the back of the embroidered paper circle. Center the smaller paper circle on top of the larger paper circle, press together, and let dry.

6. Adhere a small magnet in the center of the back of the paper brooch with two-part epoxy or other suitable glue (figure 4). Let dry.

7. To wear, hold the brooch against the garment and slide the second magnet behind the garment as shown in figure 5.

A

A

1

2

3

4

5

EMBROIDERED BROOCH

FOR THIS CREATIVE BROOCH, LAYERS OF PAPERS IN WARM, EARTHY TONES AND LINEAR, DECORATIVE STITCHING FORM AN APPEALING COMPOSITION.

MATERIALS

Decorative and/or plain papers of your choice

Photocopied design template 1

Masking tape

Waxed linen thread or embroidery thread

Polyester fiberfill

Mat board or stiff paper

Linen or cotton fabric

White craft glue

Commercial pin back

TOOLBOX

Scissors

Needle tool or slim awl

Embroidery needle, size 18

STEP BY STEP

1. Select a decorative or plain paper to use as the front layer of the brooch and another to use as the background layer.

2. Using the photocopied design template, trace the front layer of the brooch onto the selected paper and cut out with scissors. To ensure that the paper doesn't tear during stitching, cover the back of it with masking tape.

3. Using the needle tool or slim awl, pre-punch the holes for stitching in the front paper. (You can do this as you work.) Thread the embroidery needle with the waxed linen thread or embroidery thread and stitch the front of the brooch as desired, using variations in stitches and colors of thread to create interesting patterns. If you are using a decorative or patterned paper, you may want to let the design dictate where the stitches will go. If the paper is plain, you may prefer to create a simple collage and embellish it with stitches. Leave enough space around the edge of the paper for a row of stitches to attach the front piece to the background paper.

4. Cut out the background paper, making it a little larger than the stitched front piece. Lay the stitched piece on top of the background paper and pierce holes through both layers just inside the edge of the top layer all the way around. Starting at the right side, near the top of the front layer, stitch around to the top left side, forming a pocket and keeping the top open. Lightly stuff the paper pocket with polyester fiberfill, and then stitch the pocket closed.

5. Cut a piece of board (mat board or stiff paper) approximately ¼ inch (6 mm) larger than the background paper. Cut a piece of the linen or cotton fabric approximately ½ inch (1.3 cm) larger than the board.

6. Use the white glue to adhere the fabric to the board, wrapping the excess fabric to the back of the board and easing any thick areas. Glue the stitched paper brooch to the fabric-covered board and let dry.

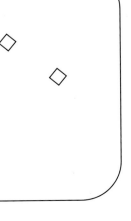

1

7. Cut a second piece of board to cover the back of the brooch that is slightly smaller than the fabric-covered board. As shown in figure 2, cut or punch two slots in the board and feed the commercial pin back through these slots. Adhere the board with the pin back to the back of the fabric-covered board with glue and let dry.

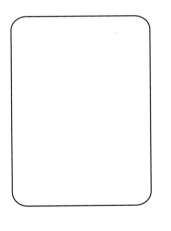

2

TRANSLUCENT TRIANGLES NECKLACE

At the heart of this design, an attractive collection of triangles lies beautifully on the neck. The sophisticated, neutral tones of the tissue paper heighten this refinement.

MATERIALS

Steel wire, 22 gauge

Tissue paper in colors of your choice

White craft glue

Sturdy string or thread of your choice

TOOLBOX

Wire snips

Flat-nose pliers

Round-nose pliers

Scissors

Small paintbrush

STEP BY STEP

1. Use your fingers to form the steel wire into whatever shapes you desire. Make as many shapes as you like. (The featured necklace has 13 triangles of varying sizes, from ½ to 1½ inches [1.3 to 3.8 cm] tall.) To straighten the wire before forming it, you can cut it into 2-foot (61 cm) lengths, hold each end in a pair of pliers, and pull them gently. Leave excess wire at the end of each shape for making loops. Gently manipulate the wires with your fingers to make sure each shape lies flat.

2. Using the excess wire, make a loop on each bent shape. To form the loop, bend one end into a small U shape. Use the flat-nose pliers to press the ends of the U together. Wrap the other end of the wire around the closed ends of the U shape several times.

3. Tear one piece of tissue paper for each wire shape. Make the paper slightly larger that the wire shape to be covered. If you prefer to have defined lines where the tissue paper overlaps, then use scissors to cut the paper instead of tearing it.

4. Dilute the white craft glue with water. Make a solution with a consistency that is more like heavy cream than honey.

5. Use the paintbrush to cover the surface of one piece of torn tissue paper with the diluted glue solution. This gets a little sticky, so have a clean damp rag on hand with which to clean your fingers.

6. Place the corresponding wire shape on the glue-covered side of the tissue paper. Smoothly wrap the edges of the tissue paper up and over the wire, pressing the edges carefully onto the back side where the paper overlaps.

7. Paint more glue on any part of the tissue paper that is not covered, and then set aside the tissue-covered wire piece to dry. To prevent the glue from sticking to any surface, either hang the piece to dry or let it dry standing up.

8. Repeat steps 5–7 for each bent-wire shape. Let all the tissue-covered wire pieces dry completely.

9. Determine the length you would like your necklace to be and cut the string or thread to this measurement. The featured necklace is 22 inches (55.9 cm) long.

10. Lay all of your bent-wire shapes on a flat surface to determine the order and spacing that you prefer. Then thread the string through the loop in the first wire piece and tie a double knot to secure it in place. Add the next wire piece ¼ to ½ inch (6 to 13 mm) from the first, and secure it with a double knot. Continue this process until all pieces are strung.

11. To wear, you can tie the ends of the string together to secure the necklace on your neck, or you can make a clasp out of the wire using the following instructions.

MAKING A SIMPLE WIRE CLASP

1. To make the hook, cut a 4-inch (10.2 cm) length of wire. Use round-nose pliers to shape a small U approximately 1 inch (2.5 cm) long in the wire.

2. Make another small U shape approximately ¼ inch (6 mm) long in the wire. This second, smaller bend should face the opposite direction from the first bend.

3. Wrap the remaining length of wire around the long tail of the first U-shaped bent wire. Bend this U over itself to make a hook.

4. Repeat steps 1–3 to make the catch, except shape the wire in step 1 more like a small O than a small U. This lets the wire catch the hook.

VELLUM & PEARL EARRINGS

DELICATE PEARL BEADS ADD THE FINISHING TOUCH TO THESE LUMINOUS EARRINGS. THE TRIO OF GRACEFUL LEAVES ARE FORMED WITH WIRE AND TRANSLUCENT VELLUM.

MATERIALS

Wire, 22 gauge, metal of your choice

Translucent white vellum

Gloss medium

2 pearl beads, ¼ inch (6 mm)

Commercial ear wires

TOOLBOX

Wire cutters

Ruler

Chain-nose pliers

Round-nose pliers

Small scissors

Smooth nonstick surface (nonstick foil or plastic laminate)

Small soft paintbrush

Floral foam or wood with predrilled holes

Very fine emery board

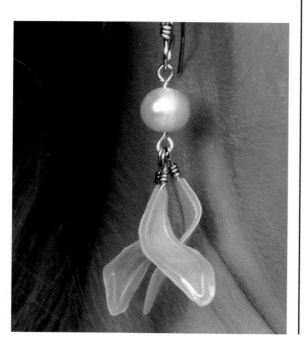

STEP BY STEP

1. Use the wire cutters to cut six 2½-inch (6.4 cm) pieces of the 22-gauge wire.

2. Use the chain-nose pliers to bend the middle of each of the wires, forming a soft V shape (figure 1). While pinching the pointed end of the bent wire in one hand, use the fingers and thumb of your other hand to gently pull and slightly curve the wire away from the point, making an organic, elongated shape (figure 2). Make sure the bent-wire frame (leaf form) is no wider than ⅜ inch (1 cm). Repeat this step to bend and shape the other five wires.

3. Measure ⅜ inch (1 cm) in from the ends of one bent-wire leaf form. Bend one end perpendicular to the other at this point (figure 3). While firmly holding the form in place at the ⅜ (1 cm) mark with round-nose pliers, grasp the end of the bent wire with chain-nose pliers and wrap it around the straight wire (figure 4). Repeat this step to wrap the end of the other five wire leaf forms.

4. Cut 12 pieces of vellum, each 1 x 1 inch (2.5 x 2.5 cm).

5. Dip one piece of the cut vellum in water for 10 to 15 seconds. Gently squeeze off the excess water between your thumb and forefinger.

6. Place the damp piece of vellum on the nonstick surface. Use a paintbrush to evenly coat one side of the paper with gloss medium.

7. Place one wire leaf form onto the coated side of the vellum, making sure the edge of the paper is just under the wrapped wire area. (Do not cover the wrapped wire with paper.)

8. Repeat step 5 with a second piece of vellum. Lay damp vellum over the leaf form, making sure not to cover the wire-wrapped area. Use your fingers to firmly press out any air bubbles, making a tight seal throughout the leaf form and

entire vellum area. Flip the vellum-covered form over on the nonstick surface and continue to press out any air bubbles, adding a thin layer of gloss medium if the vellum is drying out. The vellum must be smooth, flat, and without wrinkles or bubbles.

9. Thickly coat the vellum-covered form on both sides with gloss medium. Stand the wire end in the floral foam or in the wood with the predrilled holes. Don't let the vellum touch the foam or the wood.

10. Repeat steps 5–9 to make the other five leaf shapes. Let all of the leaves dry for one hour. Recoat all sides with gloss medium, and let dry one hour.

11. Trim the excess vellum to no less than ⅟₁₆ inch (1.6 mm) from the wire frame. Gently smooth the trimmed edges with the emery board. Using the side of your index finger, gently and slowly twist and form the leaf into shape. Coat the leaf one last time with gloss medium and let dry. (Treat the leaves gingerly after forming. Creases, cloudiness, or splitting can occur from rough contact.)

12. Using the 22-gauge wire, make two bead links for the two pearl beads. Link three of the leaf shapes to one bead link with the middle leaf facing opposite the front and back leaves. For each earring, attach the bead link to the commercial ear wire.

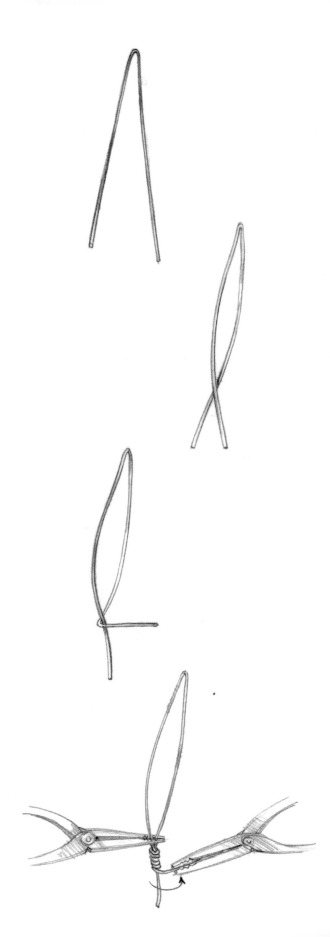

BLOOMING CHARM BRACELET

MAGAZINE IMAGES LAMINATED ON CARD STOCK ARE THE KEY ELEMENTS OF THIS SPECTACULAR BRACELET. BASE YOUR IMAGE SELECTION ON A THEME (THE DESIGNER USED FLORALS), A COLOR, OR SIMPLY CHOOSE RANDOM IMAGES THAT APPEAL TO YOU.

MATERIALS

Cover stock paper, color of your choice

Recycled magazines

White craft glue

Laminating supplies (Most print shops offer laminating services, in case you do not have a laminating machine.)

Oval link chain, sterling silver, ¼-inch (6 mm) links, 7 inches (17.8 cm) long

30 jump rings, sterling silver, each ³⁄₁₆ inch (5 mm) in diameter

Commercial clasp, sterling silver

TOOLBOX

Cutting mat

Circle cutter*

Scissors

Round hole punch, ⅛ inch (3 mm) in diameter

2 pairs of jewelry pliers

*You can substitute two large paper punches if desired, one that has a 1½-inch (3.8 cm) diameter and one with a 1-inch (2.5 cm) diameter.

STEP BY STEP

1. Place the cover stock paper on the cutting mat to protect your work surface. Use the circle cutter or a large paper punch to cut 30 circles of cover stock paper, each 1½ inches (3.8 cm) in diameter.

2. Select images you like from recycled magazines. Use the circle cutter (or a large paper punch) to cut out 30 magazine images, each 1 inch (2.5 cm) in diameter.

3. Using only a small amount of glue, carefully attach each magazine image in the center of one larger circle of cover stock paper. Make sure the glue does not wet the paper in spots, which can create bumps and blotches. The glue is simply to hold the papers in place during lamination.

4. Laminate each pair of circles. Cut out the circles from the laminated sheets, leaving a margin of about ⅛ to ¼ inch (3 to 6 mm) of plastic around each circle.

5. Determine the top of each laminated circle. Use the hole punch to make one hole approximately ⅛ inch (3 mm) away from the top edge of the circle.

6. Using jewelry pliers, attach one laminated paper circle to each link of the chain with a jump ring. Make sure each magazine image faces the same direction.

7. Secure the commercial clasp to one end of the chain. The link at the opposite end of the chain will act as the catch for the clasp.

DESIGNER
DOROTHEA HOSOM

PLYWOOD & PAPER BROOCH

THE PAPERS DECORATING THIS BROOCH ARE IN IMPECCABLE HARMONY WITH
ITS FORM. YOU CAN ADAPT THE BROOCH BY CREATING LARGER AND SMALLER
VERSIONS OR BY ADDING MORE PLYWOOD SLATS.

MATERIALS

Plywood, ⅛ inch (3 mm) thick

White craft glue

Colored magazine papers of your choice

Glue stick (optional)

Gel medium, matte

Varnish, satin finish

Two-part epoxy

2 metal posts, 18 gauge

2 scatter pin clutches

TOOLBOX

Jeweler's saw and saw blades

Ruler

Flexible shaft machine or small hand drill

Drill bit, #59 (1.04 mm)

File

Paintbrush

Wire cutters

Sandpaper

STEP BY STEP

1. Cut two pieces of ⅛-inch-thick (3 mm) plywood, each measuring 2¾ x ⅝ inch (7 x 1.6 cm).

2. Mark the center of each plywood rectangle. Using a jeweler's saw, cut a 5/16 x ⅛-inch (8 x 3 mm) slot in the center of each plywood piece.

3. Measure and mark two points on the edge of one of the slotted plywood pieces, each ½ inch (1.3 cm) in from the end. Using a #59 (1.04 mm) drill bit, drill a hole in the plywood piece at each marked point.

4. Fit the two slotted plywood pieces together so that they form a cross. (If necessary, use a small file to make minor adjustments for a better fit.) Apply a small amount of white craft glue to the joined plywood pieces and let dry.

5. Arrange the colored magazine papers on top of a white sheet of paper to create a design that complements the cross structure of the brooch. If desired, use a glue stick to temporarily keep the pieces of paper in place while you perfect your design.

6. Glue the paper cutouts to the sides, top, and ends of the plywood cross with matte gel medium. Do not apply paper to the back of the plywood brooch. Let the gel medium dry thoroughly.

7. Apply a light coat of satin-finish varnish over the paper design. Let dry.

8. On the back of the brooch, use epoxy to glue an 18-gauge metal post in each of the two holes drilled in step 3. Let dry.

9. Using wire cutters, trim each post to 5/16 inch (8 mm). Taper the end of the posts to a point with a file, and then sand smooth. Secure the brooch to clothing with scatter pin clutches.

BUTTERFLY BROOCH

DOZENS OF BUTTERFLIES, EACH ONE CUT AND SHAPED FROM HANDMADE PAPER, ARE LIGHTLY ADHERED IN A CLUSTER TO MAKE THIS STUNNING FREE-FORM BROOCH. MAKE THE CLOUD OF BUTTERFLIES THE SIZE AND SHAPE OF YOUR CHOOSING, OR VARY THE LOOK BY USING DIFFERENT COLORS AND TEXTURES OF PAPER.

MATERIALS

Scrap drawing papers or other waste papers

White craft glue

Photocopied design template 1 (optional)

Quick-drying adhesive

Sterling silver sheet, 22 gauge

Two-part epoxy

2 commercial tie tacks and clutches

TOOLBOX

Container for water

Blender

Cutting board (optional)

Plastic sheeting

Wooden rolling pin

Scissors

Scribe

Jeweler's saw and saw blades

File or sandpaper for metal

STEP BY STEP

1. Tear the scrap drawing papers and/or other waste papers into small pieces. Place the torn paper in a container of water and let them soak until they become soft.

2. Transfer the paper and some of the water into a kitchen blender and blend into a paste. Add white craft glue to the paper paste and blend.

3. Line a flat surface, such as a worktable or cutting board, with plastic. Remove the paper paste from the blender and roll it into a ball (or balls) as if you were making bread. Use the wooden rolling pin to form the paper paste into a sheet (or sheets). Make the sheet as thick as you want. Let the paper dry, and then remove the sheet from the plastic-covered surface.

4. Design a butterfly shape on paper or photocopy the design template. Cut out the original or photocopied design to use as a stencil. Trace the butterfly stencil onto the handmade paper as many times as desired. Cut out the paper butterflies with scissors. To give the butterflies dimension, wet them with water and sculpt them with your fingers. Let dry. Glue the paper butterflies together with a quick-drying adhesive.

5. Scribe the butterfly design onto the sterling silver sheet two times. Use the jeweler's saw to cut out the silver butterflies. File or sand their edges smooth. Using the two-part epoxy, glue one commercial tie tack to the back of each of the silver butterflies. Let dry. Adhere the silver butterflies to the back of the paper brooch and let dry.

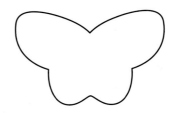

1

BAMBOO BROOCH

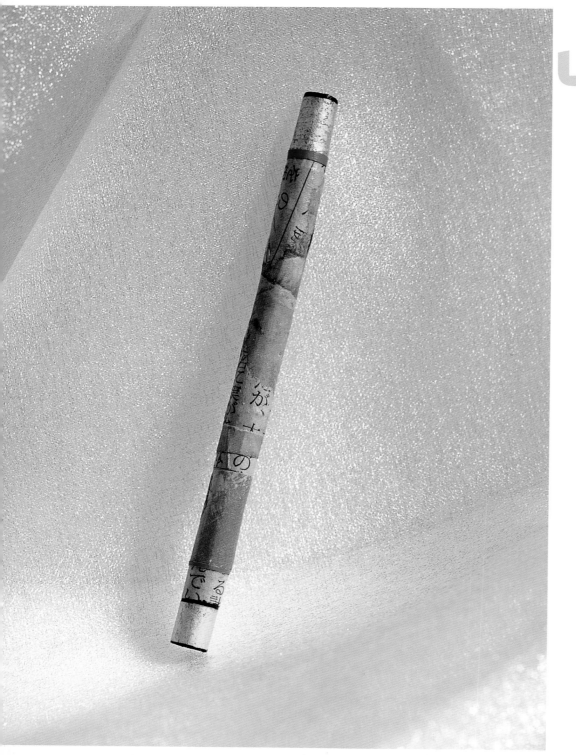

JAPANESE NEWSPRINT
AND WISPS OF
COLORED PAPER
COMBINE TO FORM
A COLLAGE THAT
IS SERENE AND
SOPHISTICATED.
THE BROOCH CAN BE
WORN VERTICALLY,
HORIZONTALLY,
OR AT ANY ANGLE
IN BETWEEN.

MATERIALS

Bamboo or wood dowel, ¼-inch (6 mm) diameter

Gel medium, matte

Japanese or other newspaper

Recycled magazines

Acrylic paint (optional)

Gold foil

Varnish, satin finish

Two-part epoxy

2 commercial wire posts, 18 gauge

2 commercial scatter pin clutches

TOOLBOX

Ruler

Jeweler's saw and saw blades

Sandpaper

Paintbrush

Scissors or craft knife

Flexible shaft machine or small hand drill

Drill bit, #59 (1.04 mm)

Wire cutters (optional)

File

STEP BY STEP

1. Measure and mark a piece of wood dowel or bamboo that is 3⅝ inches (9.2 cm) long. Use a saw to cut the dowel or bamboo to this length. Gently sand the cut ends.

2. Use a paintbrush to apply a layer of the matte gel medium to the dowel or bamboo. Adhere a layer of the Japanese newspaper to the dowel and let dry.

3. Select and cut out interesting, colorful bits of paper from recycled magazines. If you wish to achieve a distressed appearance, wet the paper and lightly rub its surface. When using a thick paper, such as from the cover of a magazine, briefly submerge it in water and peel off the back.

4. Use a paintbrush to apply the matte gel medium over the newspaper-covered dowel or bamboo. Partially cover the newspaper with bits of colored magazine papers to form a collage. Let the adhesive dry.

5. If desired, accentuate particular areas in the collage with acrylic paint and let dry.

6. Paint a thin coat of matte gel medium approximately ¼ to ⅜ inch (6 to 9.5 mm) in from each end of the dowel or bamboo. Apply gold foil over the medium and let dry.

7. Brush a light coat of satin finish matte varnish over the entire collage and let dry.

8. Determine which side of the collage will be the front of the pin. On the back of the collaged pin, measure approximately ½ inch (1.3 cm) in from each end and mark these two points. Drill a hole with the #59 (1.04-mm) bit at the marked points.

9. Use epoxy to adhere an 18-gauge wire post into each drilled hole. Let dry. With a jeweler's saw or wire cutters, trim each post to 5⁄16 inch (8 mm). Taper the cut end of the post with a file and sand smooth. Use the two scatter-pin clutches to secure the brooch to clothing.

PINWHEEL EARRINGS & RING

CAPTURE THE ENERGY OF PINWHEELS IN THIS MATCHING ORIGAMI JEWELRY SET. THE PINWHEEL DESIGNS ARE IDEAL FOR DISPLAYING TWO CONTRASTING PAPERS, WITH CRAFT WIRE FORMING BOTH THE RING BAND AND THE EAR WIRES.

MATERIALS

White craft glue

2 sheets of decorative paper in contrasting colors or styles

Photocopied design template 1

Round craft wire, 20 gauge, color of your choice

2 grommets, 1/16 inch (1.6 mm) in diameter, color of your choice

TOOLBOX

Burnisher

Scissors

Hole punch, 1/16 inch (1.6 mm) in diameter

Circle template, 3/8 inch (1 cm) in diameter

Metallic leaf pen or colored markers (optional)

Wire clippers

File

Round-nose pliers

Flat-nose pliers

Dowel or ring mandrel (for ring)

Masking tape (optional, for ring)

Dowel, 1/2 inch (1.3 cm) in diameter (for earrings)

STEP BY STEP

■ MAKING THE PINWHEEL

1. Glue the paper sheets together back to back, so the decorative sides are showing. Burnish the papers to make sure the glue is evenly distributed and the papers are secure. Let dry.

2. Trace the photocopied template, including the holes, on the decorative paper three times. Use the scissors to carefully cut out the traced templates.

3. Punch the center hole and the four corner holes in the paper form with the 1/16-inch (1.6 mm) punch.

4. Use the 3/8-inch (1 cm) circle template to trace a circle in the center of the paper form, around the punched hole. This line will be the end of each scissor cut.

5. Draw one line from the side of each punched corner hole to the 3/8-inch (1 cm) circle drawn near the center of the paper (figure 2). Each line must be drawn on the same side of each corner hole. Cut down the dotted lines with scissors, stopping at the inner circle.

6. If needed, use a metallic leaf pen or colored markers to cover the white edges of the cut paper.

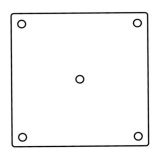

7. Cut a 6-inch (15.2 cm) piece of the 20-gauge round craft wire. File the cut ends. Coil the end of the wire around the tip of a pair of round-nose pliers for three full rotations. Make an additional half-coil. The wire is now lying across the coil (figure 3, page 64). Using flat-nose pliers, bend up the end of the half coil at a 90-degree angle (figure 4, page 64). Repeat this step twice, making a total of three coils.

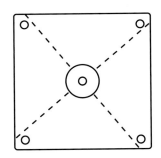

8. Thread a colored grommet onto one of the lengths of craft wire, making sure the round side or "face" of the grommet is facing the wire coil.

9. Fold the corners of the pinwheel toward the middle of the paper, align the punched holes, and thread the holes onto the wire. (The folds in the pinwheel are facing the wire coil.) Thread a second colored grommet onto the wire, making sure the round side or "face" of the grommet is facing away from the wire coil.

10. Use flat-nose pliers to bend the wire at a right angle, securing all grommets and the paper pinwheel (figure 5).

■ TO MAKE A RING

11. Determine the correct diameter for the ring size you wish to make and locate this point on a dowel or mandrel. (If needed, wrap masking tape around a dowel to create the correct size.) Wrap the excess wire around the dowel or mandrel to create the band.

12. Coil the tail of the wire around the top of the band to secure the ring (figure 6), and cut off the excess wire (figure 7).

■ TO MAKE EARRINGS

11. Place a small dowel 1 inch (2.5 cm) above the paper pinwheel and bend the excess wire over the dowel (figure 8). Reshape the wire with your fingers, if necessary. Cut off any excess wire and file the wire smooth.

12. Use flat-nose pliers to bend the ear wire at a 10-degree angle, starting approximately ¼ inch (6 mm) from its end.

MASUMI KATAOKA
Untitled, 2001
8 x 8 x 8 cm
Toilet paper, copper, imitation gold leaf;
papier-mâché

ELIANA R. ARENAS
Sweet Adornment II, 2004
Each, 5 x 10 x 5 cm
Vellum, wool, acrylic paint, polymer clay, sterling silver, magnet

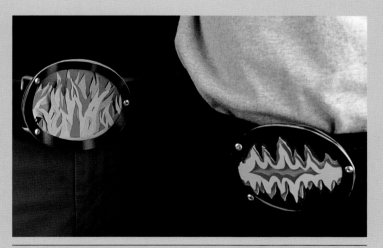

NATHAN POGLEIN
His and Hers Paper Belt Buckles, 2006
Each, 10.5 x 9 x 2 cm
Color print, construction paper,
pop rivets, aluminum tubing; hand cut

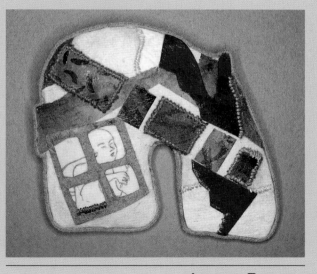

ARLENE GITOMER
Secrets, 2005
6 x 6 x 1 cm
Handmade abaca paper, gouache, thread,
batting, trapunto, paint; sewed

ART OF GEOMETRY BROOCH

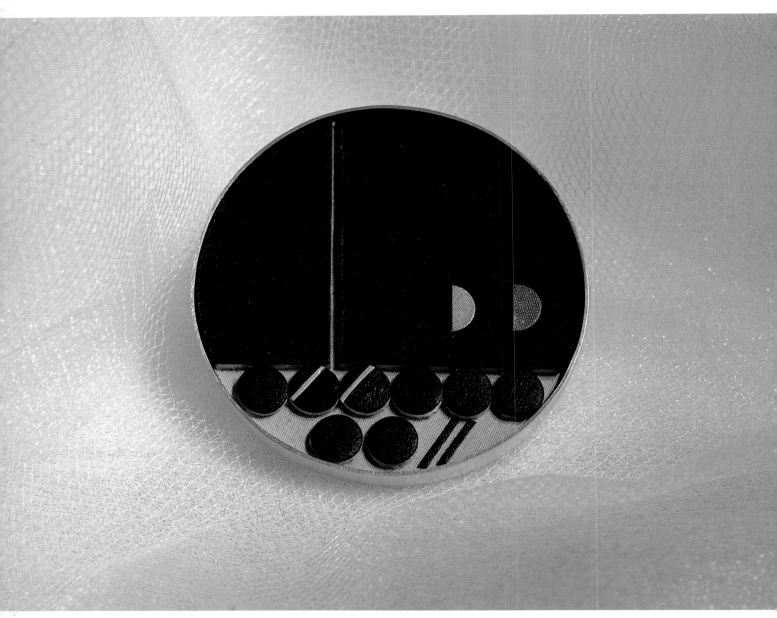

S STRONG COLORS AND BOLD GRAPHIC FORMS MAKE THIS BROOCH ABSOLUTELY MODERN. THICK MAT BOARD MIXED WITH THIN MAGAZINE PAPER PRODUCES AN AMAZING AMOUNT OF DEPTH. YOU CAN EASILY MODIFY THIS PROJECT BY CHANGING THE SHADES AND SHAPES.

MATERIALS

Acrylic sheet, ¹⁄₁₆ inch (1.6 mm) thick

Acrylic paint, black

Recycled magazine papers, yellows and black

Gel medium, matte

Photocopied design template 1

Mat board, black

Varnish, satin finish

Commercial pin back, self-adhesive

TOOLBOX

Ruler

Jeweler's saw and saw blades

Sandpaper

Paintbrush

Small sharp scissors

Standard hole punch

STEP BY STEP

1. Measure and mark a circle on the acrylic sheet that is 1½ inches (3.8 cm) in diameter. Cut out the circle with a jeweler's saw. Sand the edge and the top surface of the acrylic circle with sandpaper.

2. Using a paintbrush, apply black acrylic paint to the sanded surfaces and let dry.

3. Measure and mark a circle on a yellow magazine page that is 1½ inches (3.8 cm) in diameter. Cut out the paper circle and glue it to the acrylic circle with the matte gel medium. Let dry.

4. Transfer the photocopied design template onto the black mat board. Cut out these two shapes with the jeweler's saw.

5. Punch eight circles from the black mat board with the standard hole punch.

6. Using the hole punch, punch out two yellow circles and a black circle from the recycled magazine pages. Use the small sharp scissors to cut the black circle in half.

7. Cut two yellow and two black magazine-paper strips, each approximately ¹⁄₃₂ x ¼ inch (0.8 x 6 mm).

8. With the matte gel medium, glue the paper and the mat board shapes on the 1½-inch (3.8 cm) circle according to the design illustrated in figure 2. Let dry.

9. Using the paintbrush, apply a layer of satin-finish varnish to the top of the paper cutout design and let dry.

10. Attach a self-adhesive commercial pin back to the back of the brooch.

DESIGN IDEA

■ After completing the design, use basic metalworking skills to set the collaged acrylic circle in a bezel. You can also attach handmade pin findings or scatter pins to the back of the bezel.

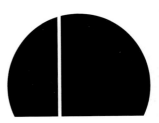

1

2

DECOUPAGE EARRINGS & BRACELET

DESIGNER
JAMES BOVÉ

ECHOING THE SHAPE OF PAPER LANTERNS, THESE DELICATE EARRINGS WILL ALWAYS BE IN FASHION. PAIR THEM WITH A MATCHING BRACELET FOR A SUITE OF SENSATIONAL STYLE.

MATERIALS

Wire, metal and gauge of your choice

Commercial wire shapes of your choice (optional, for earrings)

Plain or decorative tissue papers

Decoupage medium

Corrugated cardboard

Ear wires, commercial or handmade (for earrings)

TOOLBOX

Wire cutters

Pliers

Paper bag or cardboard box

Spray adhesive

Paintbrush

STEP BY STEP

■ MAKING THE EARRINGS

1. Begin with the wire bases. They may be flat or dimensional, but be sure to consider how the earrings will hang. Find interesting shapes at a local craft store or create your own by manipulating the wire with your fingers or with pliers. Make sure there is a loop at the top of each wire shape to connect to the ear wire.

2. Using a paper bag or a cardboard box as your spray booth, spray an even layer of spray adhesive on one side of the tissue paper and let dry.

3. Tear small strips from the tissue paper and stretch over the wire framework. With one layer in place, use a watered-down mixture of the decoupage medium to secure it. Allow this layer to dry.

4. After the base layer is secure, experiment with your design and add other layers and colors of paper. You can add as many layers as you need in order to achieve the look you want. Be sure to allow drying time before adding each new layer. If you prefer a more transparent look, just layer on the decoupage glue for strength instead of adding more paper.

5. Repeat steps 2–4 to make the second earring. Use pliers to attach one ear wire to each earring.

■ MAKING THE BRACELET

1. Bend the wire around your wrist to determine the preferred shape and size for the bracelet. Explore space with the wire by winding it back on itself. Secure the end of the wire, twisting it around itself or binding it with other wire (figure 1).

2. To cover the wire with paper, follow steps 2–4 of Making the Earrings.

1

TALISMAN PENDANT

L LAYERS OF ATTRACTIVE HANDMADE PAPERS ARE ENHANCED WITH BOTH

FUNCTIONAL AND PURELY DECORATIVE STITCHING TO ADD COLOR AND

DEPTH TO THIS AMULET-STYLE NECKPIECE.

MATERIALS

Plain or decorative papers of your choice

Photocopied design template 1

Masking tape

Waxed linen thread or embroidery thread

Polyester fiberfill

Necklace cord of your choice

TOOLBOX

Scissors

Needle tool or slim awl

Embroidery needle, size 18

Ruler

STEP BY STEP

1. Select plain or decorative papers of your choice for the neckpiece. If desired, layer several papers to create a collage. Using the photocopied design template, trace the pattern on the selected papers and cut out with scissors. If desired, you can change the scale of the template to make a larger or smaller piece.

2. To ensure that the paper doesn't tear during stitching, cover the back of it with masking tape.

3. Leaving a margin on the edge to stitch the piece closed, use the needle tool or slim awl to pre-punch holes for stitching. Thread the embroidery needle with the waxed linen thread or embroidery thread and stitch as desired, using variations in stitches and colors of thread to create interesting patterns. If you are using a decorative or patterned paper, you may want to let the design dictate where the stitches will go.

4. Fold the paper as indicated by line A on the design template and stitch the two sides together, leaving the top open.

5. Lightly stuff with fiberfill, and then fold the top down (line B) and tuck it into the pocket. Stitch closed.

6. Fold the top flap (line C) to create a tube for the cord. Measure and cut a piece of cord 30 inches (76.2 cm) long, or to your desired length. Thread the cord through the tube and tie the ends together. Arrange the cord so the tied ends are concealed inside the tube.

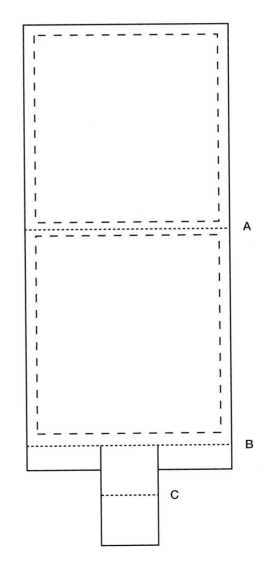

CUT, CLARITY, COLOR, CARAT

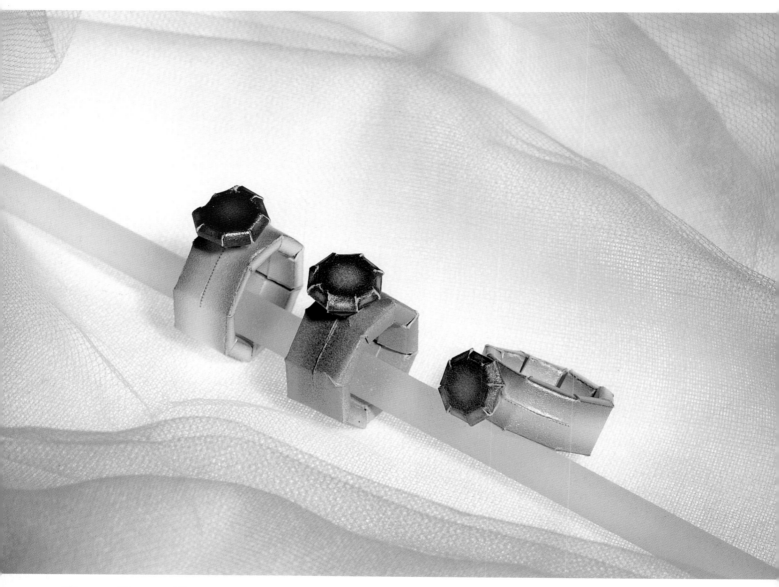

WHAT COULD BE MORE FUN THAN WEARING A HUGE PAPER DIAMOND
SOLITAIRE FOR ALL YOUR FRIENDS TO ADMIRE? AFTER FOLDING A FEW
PRACTICE RINGS, YOU'LL BE SETTING THESE PAPER STONES IN A JIFFY.

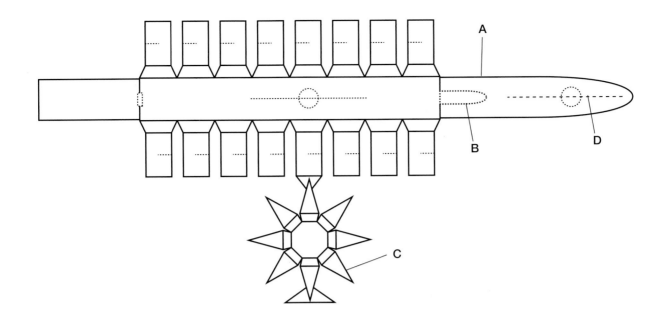

MATERIALS

Photocopied design template 1

Paper of your choice for the ring

TOOLBOX

Sharp craft knife

STEP BY STEP

1. Use the sharp knife to cut out the photo-copied design template. Cut slits in the paper on the dotted lines.

2. As shown in figure 2, fold A inward, leaving B pointing out.

3. As shown in figures 3 and 4, insert the diamond shape C through D from the bottom.

4. Turn over the paper (figure 5, page 74). Using the lines as a guide, fold and unfold all the tabs to crease.

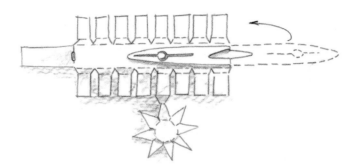

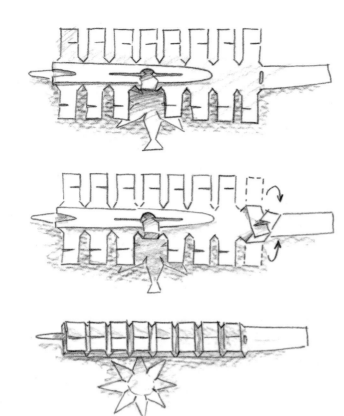

5. Starting on either side of the ring, lock two opposite tabs as shown in figure 6. Repeat this process until all the tabs are locked (figure 7).

6. Turn over the ring. To close the ring, fold the paper into a circle with the locked tabs on the inside (figure 8).

7. Insert tab E into tab F (figure 8). Insert tab G into tab H (figure 9).

8. Fold the diamond shape with the colored side of the paper facing out (figure 10). Tuck the diamond corners and tab I into the hole on the ring's surface (figure 11).

KATHY BUSZKIEWICZ
Omnia Vanitas IX, 2004
3.8 x 4.4 x 4.4 cm
U.S. currency, 18-karat gold, pearl;
hand fabricated, pieced
PHOTOS © ARTIST

RACHEL N. MILLS
Untitled, 2005
11.4 x 139 cm
Telephone book pages, copper wire, pearls;
hand woven, mold formed, threaded
PHOTO © NATALYA PINCHUCK

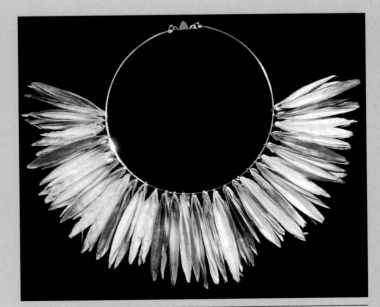

LISA M. WILSON
Husk Collar, 2006
19 x 19 cm
Ogura lace paper, parchment, sterling silver
PHOTO © ARTIST

FRENCH KNOTS & CROSSES NECKLACE

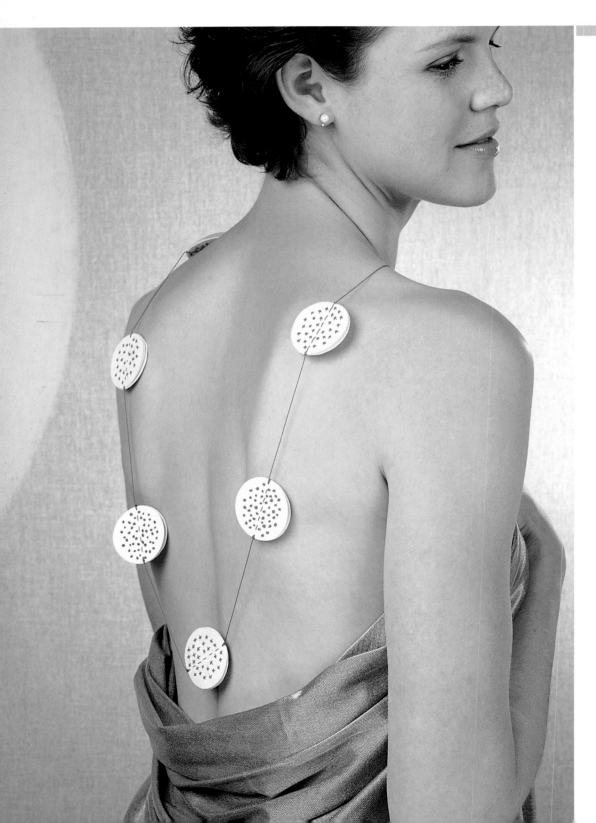

THE CIRCLE IS A SYMBOLIC FORM PUT TO GOOD USE IN THIS POETIC NECKLACE. STACKED LAYERS OF CREAM-COLORED PAPER ARE SEWN WITH RED SILK THREAD TO FORM AN ENCHANTING CHAIN.

MATERIALS

Heavy handmade paper or watercolor paper

Washi paper

Silk thread, red, 0.018 inch (0.45 mm) in diameter, 15.3 yards (14 m)

White craft glue

Silk thread, red, 0.020 inch (0.50 mm) in diameter, 2.2 feet (2 m)

TOOLBOX

Cutting mat

Ruler

Circle cutter

Large needle or awl

Embroidery needle

Scissors

MAKING A FRENCH KNOT STITCH

(Can be worked in any direction.)

As shown in figure 1, bring the needle up at point A. Hold the thread taut with the finger and thumb of your nondominant hand. Tightly wind the thread once or twice (not more) around the needle tip.

Still holding the thread, insert the needle close to point A and pull it through to the back of the work (figure 2), so the twists lie on the fabric surface neatly. Repeat as required.

A

MAKING A KNOTTED CROSS STITCH

Work over an imaginary cross. As shown in figure 3, make a vertical stitch, and then bring the needle through at the right arm of the cross.

Work a horizontal stitch across the first stitch, looping it to make a knot at the center without picking up the fabric (figures 4 and 5).

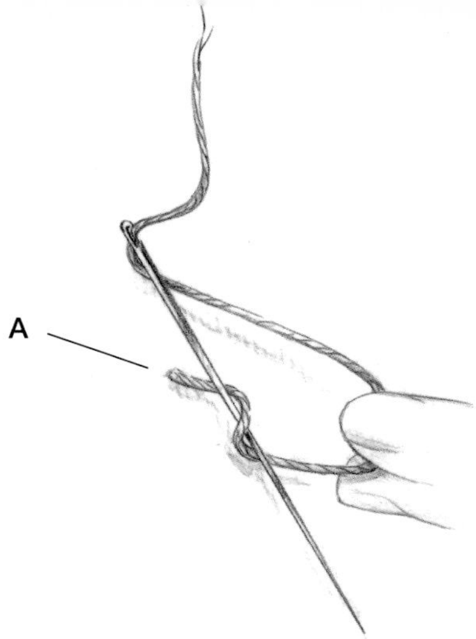

1

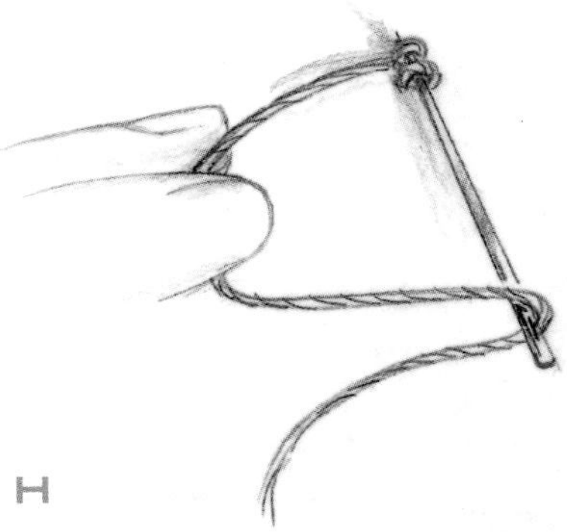

2

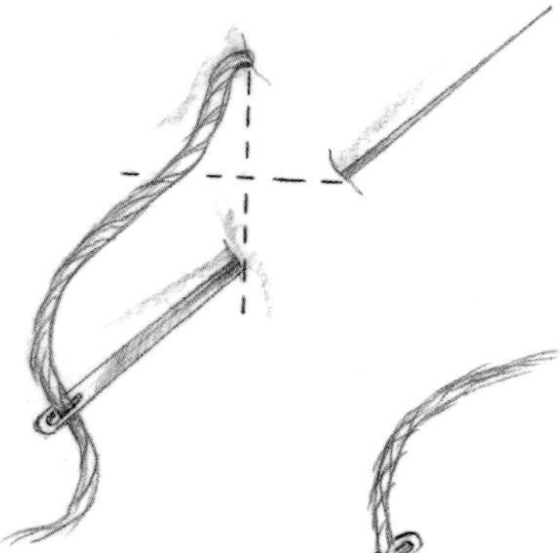

3

4

5

STEP BY STEP

1. Place the heavy handmade or watercolor paper on top of the cutting mat. Use the circle cutter to cut 14 circles out of the paper, each 1 11/16 inches (4.2 cm) in diameter. Cut 21 circles out of the washi paper, each 1 9/16 inches (4 cm) in diameter.

2. Using the thinner red silk thread and the awl and needle, embroider eight of the heavyweight paper circles with knotted crosses. Embroider the remaining six heavyweight circles with French knots.

3. Make seven stacks of washi-paper circles with three circles in each stack. To hold each group of three circles together, dab a little glue in the center of the paper circles and let dry. (This keeps the circles from moving when they are pierced.)

4. Pick up four knotted-cross circles and three French-knot circles. Slide each circle under a stack of washi-paper circles with the embroidery facing down. Place one embroidered circle on top of each pile with the stitching facing up, matching the type of stitches on the top and bottom circles for each stack. You should now have seven stacks, each with matching embroidered circles on the top and bottom and three washi-paper circles sandwiched in the middle.

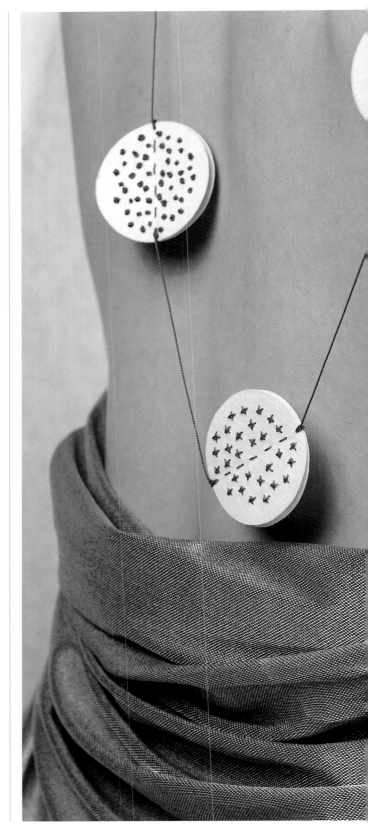

5. Transfer one stack of paper circles onto a cutting mat and firmly hold them together. Use the needle to pierce 12 equally spaced holes through the stacked paper across the diameter of the circle (figure 6). Be sure to hold the stack securely so it does not move. Repeat this step for the other six stacks of paper.

6. Unroll the thicker red silk thread, and thread it through a needle. Position each stack of paper circles so the pierced holes are aligned. (You can check the alignment by holding the paper to a light.)

7. Start stitching the paper circles together, beginning with a knotted-cross stack (figure 7). As you stitch, knot the thread at the start and the end of each circle's diameter to close the stack as shown in figure 8. (If you prefer an open look to the stacks, you can leave the sides unknotted.) Space the circles approximately 3½ inches (8.9 cm) apart. Alternate the knotted-cross embellished circle stacks with the French-knot embellished circle stacks.

8. After sewing the last stack, measure approximately 8 inches (20.3 cm) of thread to create a length on the necklace to wear across the back of the neck. Knot and cut the thread at this point. Hide the end knot inside the first paper stack, between its layers (figure 9). Grab the other end of the thread and thread it on a needle. Knot the thread to the last stitch on the edge of the last circle stack, cut and hide the end as previously done inside the stack. Glue the ends in between the paper layers to secure them.

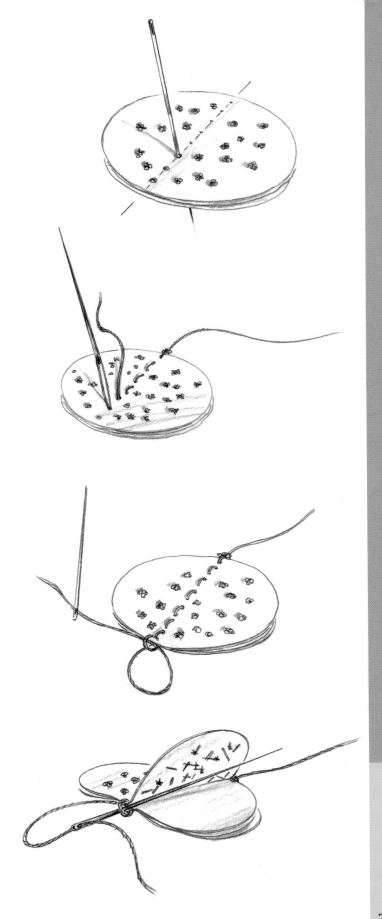

INTERLOCKING NECKLACE & BRACELET

YUMMY PASTEL COLORS MAKE THIS NECKLACE AND BRACELET SET A TREAT. SURPRISINGLY, IT'S CREATED FROM DYED POLYETHYLENE-FIBER ENVELOPES WHICH WORK UP EASILY AS A LONG NECKLACE OR BROAD BRACELET.

■ FOR THE NECKLACE

MATERIALS

High-density polyethylene-fiber envelopes

Permanent pigments (inks, dyes, markers, paints, or pencils) in colors of your choice (optional)

Photocopied design template 1 (A, B, C, and D)

White craft glue

Wire, 18 gauge or thicker (optional, for clasp)

TOOLBOX

Craft knife

Wire cutters (optional, for clasp)

File (optional, for clasp)

Round-nose pliers (optional, for clasp)

STEP BY STEP

1. If desired, alter the color of the polyethylene-fiber envelopes before or after cutting out the links (step 2). Any permanent pigment will work. Ink works especially well, because it exposes the polyethylene fibers. Many dyes, markers, paints, and pencils also color the material nicely. Experiment with stickers and the marks that are already on recycled polyethylene-fiber envelopes, such as postage and postmark stamps.

2. Cut out 12 pieces of polyethylene-fiber sheets, each 15/16 x 3⅛ inches (2.4 x 8 cm). Cut out 12 additional pieces, each 15/16 x 7 inches (2.4 x 17.8 cm).

3. Transfer the photocopied design templates onto the polyethylene-fiber sheets. Trace 11 small links (A), 12 large links (B), one small sliced link (C), and two connector forms (D). Use a craft knife to cut out the forms.

4. Take one small link and bend it slightly to form a U shape. Align the two round openings located at the ends of the link. Feed one end of a second, large link through these round openings diagonally. Pull the second link halfway through the openings, and form a U shape with this link.

5. Repeat step 4 to join all of the small and large links. Attach the sliced link last. (The sliced link and connector forms will be used to join the last link with the first link and close the necklace.)

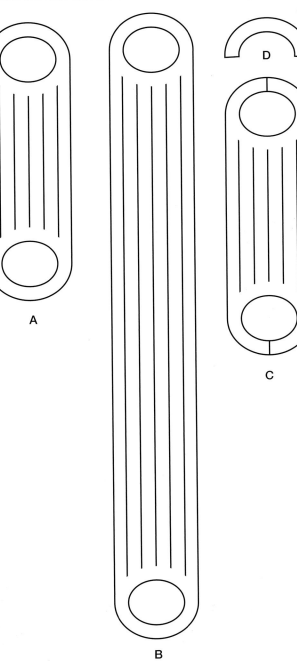

A

B

C

D

6. Use glue to adhere the end of one connector to one side of the opening in the sliced link. Thread the connector under the strands of the first link. Glue the other end of the connector to the sliced link. Repeat this step on the other end of the sliced link. Let the glue dry.

7. Wear the necklace long if you wish, or double it and join the links with a simple clasp. To make a simple clasp, cut approximately 2⅜ inches (6 cm) of wire that is 18 gauge or thicker. File the cut wire ends flat. Using round-nose pliers, curve one end back onto the wire, making a tight circle, or loop. Curve the other end of the wire in the opposite direction, forming a second tight circle or loop. The wire now has loops on both ends. Feed the wire through the round openings in two small links. Use round-nose pliers to carefully bend the wire into a tight S shape.

A

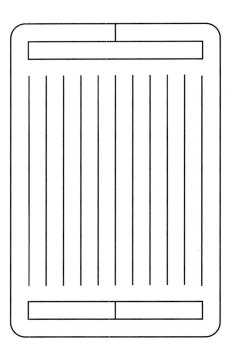

B

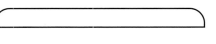

C

■ FOR THE WIDE BRACELET

MATERIALS

High-density polyethylene-fiber envelopes, enough for six 2⅜ x 3½-inch (6 x 9 cm) pieces

Permanent pigments (inks, dyes, markers, paints, or pencils) in colors of your choice (optional)

Photocopied design template 2 (A, B, and C)

White craft glue

TOOLBOX

Craft knife

STEP BY STEP

1. You can alter the color of the polyethylene-fiber sheets before or after cutting out the links. (For details on how to do this, see step 1 for the necklace.) Transfer photocopied template A (link form) onto the sheet five times. Transfer photocopied template B (sliced link form) onto the sheet once. Transfer photocopied template C (connector form) onto the sheet two times. Use a craft knife to cut out these shapes.

2. Take one link form and slightly bend it into a U shape. Align the openings located near the ends of the form. Feed a second link form diagonally through the openings and pull it halfway through the openings. Form a U shape with the second link form.

3. Repeat step 2 five times, using the sliced link form last.

4. Glue the end of one connector to one side of the opening in the sliced link. Thread the connector through the strands of the first bracelet link. Glue the other end of the connector to the last link. Repeat this step to attach the second connector to the other end of the sliced link.

NATURE-IN-PAPER BROOCHES

A BIRD. A LEAF. A FLOWER. WHO HASN'T BEEN INSPIRED BY THESE NATURAL WONDERS? CELEBRATE THEM WITH A TRIO OF FANCIFUL PAPER BROOCHES EMBELLISHED WITH EYELETS AND RIBBON.

MATERIALS

■ FOR THE BIRD

Photocopied design templates 1, 2, and 3 (page 86)

Decorative papers, each 4 x 3 inches (10.2 x 7.6 cm), in plum, mauve mulberry, and blue

Decorative papers, each 2 inches (5.1 cm) square, pink mulberry and sheet music pattern

Decorative paper, ½ inch (1.3 cm) square, copper colored

Silver eyelet, 1/16 inch (1.6 mm) in diameter

Pink ribbon, 3 inches (7.6 cm) long

Commercial pin back, 1½ inches (3.8 cm) long

Industrial-strength adhesive

■ FOR THE LEAF

Twig, 1¾ inches (4.4 cm) long

Copper paint

Photocopied design templates 4, 5, 6, and 7 (pages 86 and 87)

Map paper, 3 inches (7.6 cm) square

Decorative papers in kelly green, blue, and chartreuse, each 3 inches (7.6 cm) square

Metallic gold paper, 2 x 3 inches (5.1 x 7.6 cm)

Commercial pin back, 1½ inches (3.8 cm) long

Industrial-strength adhesive

■ FOR THE FLOWER

Photocopied design templates 8 and 9 (page 88)

Red paper, 3 inches (7.6 cm) square

Purple paper, 1 x ⅞ inch (2.5 x 2.2 cm)

Printed paper, gold and red, 1½ inches (3.8 cm) square

Brass eyelet, ⅛ inch (3 mm)

Commercial pin back, ¾ inch (1.9 cm) long

Industrial-strength adhesive

TOOLBOX

Scissors

Glue stick

Laminating machine and 0.02-mm-thick plastic laminating pouches (Most print shops offer laminating services if you do not have a machine.)

Round hole punch, 1/16 inch (1.6 mm)

Permanent marker

Eyelet setter

Small mallet

Sandpaper

Paintbrush

Standard hole punch

Round hole punch, ⅛ inch (3 mm)

STEP BY STEP

■ BIRD BROOCH

1. Trace photocopied design template 1 onto the plum paper. Trace the same template onto the mauve mulberry paper. With the scissors, cut out the two bird shapes. Use the glue stick to tack the mulberry bird on top of the plum bird.

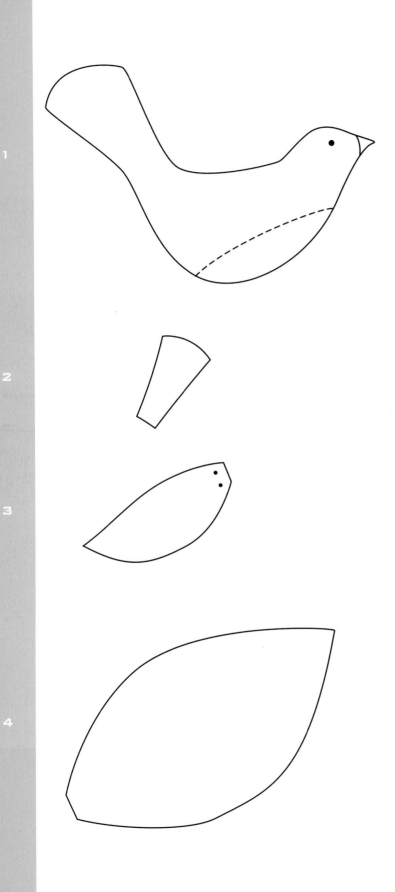

2. Trace photocopied design template 1 onto the blue paper. When cutting out the bird shape, cut down the dotted breast line. Use the glue stick to tack the blue bird shape into place.

3. Trace the tail feathers (template 2) onto the mauve mulberry paper and cut out. Center this piece at the top of the bird's tail and tack in place with glue stick.

4. Cut three thin strips of plum paper, each ¹⁄₂₅ x 1 inch (1 x 25 mm). Glue plum paper strips on top of the mauve tail feather piece so that they fan outward.

5. Slide the assembled paper bird into a laminating pouch and laminate the form.

6. Trace template 3, the wing shape, onto the pink mulberry paper and again onto the sheet music. Cut out both wing shapes, and then glue the mulberry paper on top of the sheet music.

7. Cut a small triangle from the copper-colored paper for the bird's beak.

8. Slide the wing and the beak into a laminating pouch and laminate these forms.

9. Trim around all of the laminated paper shapes, leaving a small border of clear plastic film.

10. Punch two ¹⁄₁₆-inch (1.6 mm) holes in the square end of the wing. Align the wing on top of the body. Using the wing holes as a guide, punch two holes through the body of the laminated paper bird.

11. Mark a point for the bird's eye with a permanent marker. Punch a hole at the marked point using the ¹⁄₁₆-inch (1.6 mm) punch. Thread the silver eyelet through the hole. Turn the bird over onto a hard work surface. Secure the eyelet with an eyelet setter.

12. Thread one end of the pink ribbon down through the front side of the bird's wing and body. Bring the ribbon back up through the two laminated-paper layers, tie the loose ends in a snug knot, and then trim the ends of the ribbon.

13. Lightly sand the tip of the beak on the laminated bird form and the back of the copper beak. Glue the copper beak onto the bird form with industrial-strength adhesive and let dry.

14. Sand the back of the commercial pin back. Lightly sand the back of the bird where the pin back will be affixed (centered just above the middle of the bird). Glue the pin back in place with industrial-strength adhesive and let dry.

■ LEAF BROOCH

1. Paint the twig with the copper paint. Set it aside to dry.

2. Trace photocopied design template 4, the whole leaf shape, onto the map paper and cut out.

3. Trace photocopied design template 5, one side of the leaf, onto the kelly green paper. Trace this shape again onto the blue paper. Cut out both traced shapes.

4. Using a standard hole punch, punch random holes into the kelly green paper cut in step 3 or punch holes at the locations marked on the template with an X. Use a glue stick to tack the kelly green punched paper piece on top of the blue piece.

5. Using photocopied design template 6, trace the second side of the leaf onto the chartreuse paper. Cut out the traced form.

6. Align the chartreuse paper cutout on top of the right side of the whole leaf shape (map paper). Tack these elements in place with a glue stick.

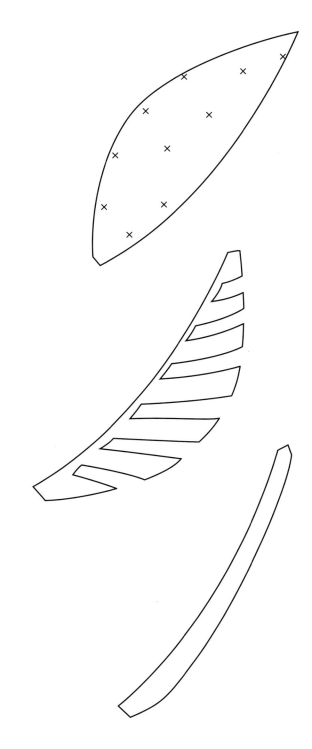

7. Position the kelly green and blue paper cutout on top of the left side of the whole leaf shape and tack in place with a glue stick.

8. Using photocopied design template 7, trace the arch shape onto the gold paper and cut out. Glue this piece directly over the middle seam of the leaf, where the two sides join.

9. Slide the paper leaf into the laminate pouch and laminate it. Trim around the paper shape, leaving a small border of clear plastic film.

10. Lightly sand the back of the leaf where the pin back and twig will be affixed. Sand the back of the commercial pin back.

11. Determine how you want the leaf brooch to lay on the wearer, and attach the pin back accordingly with industrial-strength adhesive. Place a small amount of adhesive on the back of the leaf shape, near the bottom, and attach the painted twig. Let the glue dry.

■ FLOWER BROOCH

1. Using photocopied design template 8, trace the flower pattern onto the red paper and cut out.

2. Cut six thin strips from the purple paper, each ⅞ inch (2.2 cm) long. Use a glue stick to tack one purple strip to the center of each flower petal. Slide the red paper flower into a laminate pouch and laminate.

3. Using photocopied design template 9, trace the center of the flower onto the printed gold and red paper and cut out. Slide this piece of paper into a laminate pouch and laminate it.

4. Trim around both laminated paper shapes, leaving a small border of clear plastic film.

5. Find and mark the center of the gold paper circle. Using the ⅛-inch (3 mm) hole punch, punch a hole for the brass eyelet at this point. Center the gold circle on top of the red paper flower. Using the hole in the gold circle as a guide, punch a matching hole in the red paper flower. Thread the brass eyelet through the two layers of laminated paper and turn the flower over onto a hard work surface. Secure the eyelet with an eyelet setter.

6. Lightly sand the back of the paper flower where the pin back will be attached (above the eyelet). Sand the back of the commercial pin back. Glue the pin back in place using the industrial-strength adhesive and let dry.

ANIKA SMULOVITZ
Choker from *The Chocolate Series*, 2002
16.4 x 16.4 x 4.4 cm
Chocolate wrappers, brass, wood clasp;
hand fabricated, soldered, carved, riveted
PHOTO © ARTIST

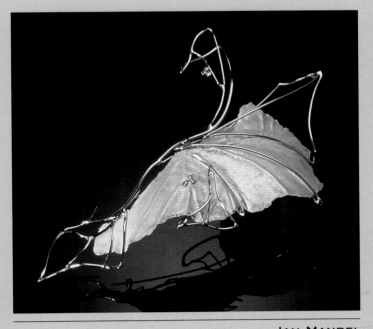

JAN MANDEL
Winter Solstice—Ghost Leaf Series, 2005
16.5 x 8 x 3.5 cm
18-karat yellow gold, paper, diamonds, lacquer
PHOTO © FREDDIE LIEBERMAN

KATJA TOPORSKI
Snow, 2006
7 x 5 x 4 cm
Vellum, sterling silver wire;
fabricated
PHOTO © ARTIST

ANDREA SHAVLIK
Untitled, 2006
2.5 x 6.5 x 3 cm
Rolled paper, sterling silver
PHOTO © YUKO YAGISAWA

ETHEREAL LEAF EARRINGS

DESIGNER
CYNTHIA WULLER

SHEER LUXURY. THESE LIGHT-WEIGHT EARRINGS ARE EFFORTLESS TO WEAR AND EASY TO MAKE. USE TRADITIONAL DECOUPAGE TECHNIQUES TO ADHERE VELLUM SHEETS TO A WIRE FRAME FOR AN EFFECT THAT IS UP-TO-THE-MINUTE CHIC.

MATERIALS

Wire, 24 gauge

Translucent white vellum

Gloss medium

Commercial ear wires

TOOLBOX

Ruler

Wire cutters

Chain-nose pliers

Round-nose pliers

Small scissors

Smooth nonstick surface (nonstick foil or plastic laminate)

Small soft paintbrush

Floral foam or wood block with predrilled holes

Emery board, very fine

STEP BY STEP

1. **Option A:** To make large leaf earrings, use the wire cutters to cut two 6-inch (15.2 cm) pieces and two 2-inch (5.1 cm) pieces of the 24-gauge wire. Set aside the 2-inch (5.1 cm) pieces for the leaf veins.

Option B: To make small leaf earrings, use the wire cutters to cut two 4-inch (10.2 cm) pieces and two 1⅛-inch (2.9 cm) pieces of the 24-gauge wire. Set aside the 1⅛-inch (2.9 cm) pieces for the leaf veins.

2. Use the chain-nose pliers to bend the middle of one of the longer wires, forming a soft V shape (figure 1). While pinching the pointed end of the bent wire in one hand, use your fingers and thumb of the other hand to gently pull and slightly curve the wire away from the point, making an organic, elongated shape (figure 2). Make sure that the bent-wire frame (leaf form) is no wider than ⅜ inch (1 cm). Repeat this step to bend the second long wire.

3. Measure ⅜ inch (1 cm) in from the ends of one bent-wire leaf form. Bend one end perpendicular to the other at this point (figure 3, page 92). While firmly holding the form in place at the ⅜-inch (1 cm) mark with round-nose pliers, grasp the end of the bent wire with chain-nose pliers and wrap it around the straight wire (figure 4, page 92). Repeat this step to wrap the end of the second wire leaf form.

4. If you are making the large leaf earrings, use the scissors to cut four 1 x 3-inch (2.5 x 7.6 cm) pieces of vellum. If you are making the small leaf earrings, cut four 1 x 2-inch (2.5 x 5.1 cm) vellum pieces.

5. Dip one piece of the cut vellum in water for 10 to 15 seconds. Gently squeeze off the excess water between your thumb and forefinger.

6. Place the damp piece of vellum on the nonstick surface. Use a paintbrush to evenly coat one side of the paper with gloss medium.

1

2

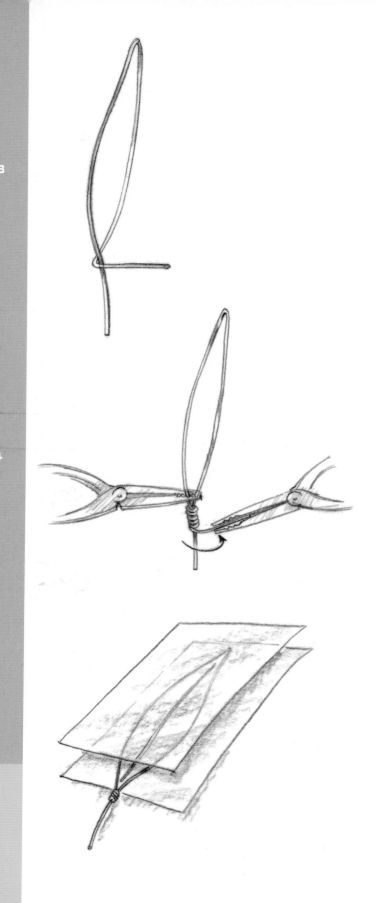

7. Place one wire leaf form onto the coated side of the vellum, making sure the edge of the paper is just under the wrapped wire area. (Do not cover the wrapped wire with paper.) Place the leaf-vein wire on the coated vellum in the center of the leaf form.

8. Repeat step 5 with a second piece of vellum. Lay damp vellum over the leaf form, making sure not to cover the wire-wrapped area (figure 5). Use your fingers to firmly press out any air bubbles, making a tight seal throughout the leaf form and entire vellum area. Flip the leaf over on the nonstick surface and continue to press out any air bubbles, adding a thin layer of gloss medium if the vellum is drying out. The vellum must be smooth, flat, and without wrinkles or bubbles.

9. Thickly coat the vellum-covered leaf form on both sides with gloss medium. Stand the leaf's wire end in the floral foam or in the wood with the predrilled holes. Don't let the vellum touch the foam or wood.

10. Repeat steps 5–9 to make a second earring. Let both leaves dry for one hour. Recoat all sides with gloss medium, and let dry one hour.

11. Trim the excess vellum to no less than ¹⁄₁₆ inch (1.6 mm) from the wire frame. Gently smooth the trimmed edges with the emery board. Using the side of your index finger, gently and slowly twist and form the leaf into shape. Coat the leaf one last time with gloss medium and let dry. (Treat the leaves gingerly after forming. Creases, cloudiness, or splitting can occur from rough contact.)

12. Form a loop in the wire at the top of both leaves, and attach commercial ear wires.

AMI AVELLÁN
Green, Green Grass of Home, 2006
130 x 13 cm
Wallpaper, paper string, glass beads,
bookbinder's canvas
PHOTO © ARTIST

SASKIA BOSTELMANN
Post It...to Me, 2006
Each, 2.5 x 11 cm
Self-adhesive notes, gouache, metallic ink, cardboard,
sterling silver pins; folded, glued
PHOTO © ARTIST

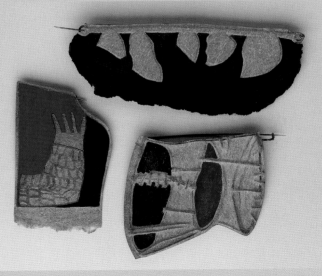

BEATE EISMANN
3 Brooches, 2003
Top, 7.5 x 20 x 1.5 cm;
bottom left, 11 x 7.8 x 0.9 cm;
bottom right, 11.3 x 10 x 1.6 cm
Asparagus paper, silver, paint;
hand fabricated
PHOTO © HELGA SCHULZE-BRINKOP

GOLD LEAF WISP PINS

COMBINE THE
GLEAM OF GOLD
AND SILVER WITH
THE FLOWING
CURVE OF STEMS
AND LEAF SHAPES
TO MAKE THESE
VERSATILE AND
ENCHANTING
STICKPINS.

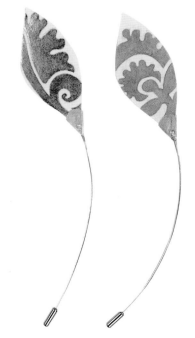

MATERIALS

Photocopied design template 1, A, B, or C

Watercolor paper or card stock, off-white or cream

White craft glue

Gouache, red

Gold and/or silver leaf

Fine silver sheet, 28 gauge

Sterling silver wire, hard, 19 gauge

Stickpin catches

TOOLBOX

Tracing paper

Cutting mat

Craft knife

Small paintbrush, pointed tip

Rubber band

Burnisher (agate burnisher works best for leafing)

Glassine paper

Paintbrush, soft bushy tip

Double-sided tape

Jeweler's saw and saw blades

File

Riveting hammer

Steel block

Center punch

Flexible shaft machine or small hand drill

Drill bit, 0.04 inch (0.9 mm)

Sandpapers

Radial brush, 400 grit

Half-round needle file

Needle (optional)

BEFORE YOU BEGIN

The following directions are for creating a single pin. Repeat each step as you go along to make multiple pins.

STEP BY STEP

■ MAKING THE PAPER LEAVES

1. Use tracing paper and a pencil to transfer the photocopied design template onto the watercolor paper or card stock. Transfer the outline of the leaf and its interior pattern (A, B, or C). On a cutting mat, cut out the leaf with a craft knife. Use a flowing movement so the cut is natural and clean.

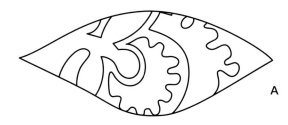

A

B

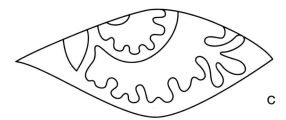

C

2. Mix an equal-parts solution of white craft glue and water. Add a very small dab of red gouache to the solution. (This will slightly color the glue mixture and will help you see where you have painted it.) Using the small brush, paint the glue mixture inside the pattern (figure 2). Let the glue dry for 30 minutes. Paint a second layer, and let it dry for 30 minutes. Paint a third layer, and let dry one hour.

3. Roll a scrap piece of card stock or watercolor paper into a small tube and secure it with a rubber band (figure 3). Have a transfer gold leaf ready to use. Blow through the cardboard tube and over the paper leaf. The

steam from your breath will make the layers of glue tacky. Place the gold leaf on top of the paper leaf (figure 4) and rub it with your fingernail or a burnisher. Lift the gold leaf, place a piece of glassine paper on top, and burnish it again to help the gold leaf adhere to the paper. Brush off the particles that do not adhere with a soft brush. If more gold needs to be applied, repeat the procedure.

■ MAKING THE METAL BASE

4. Place a piece of tracing paper on top of the paper leaf and trace the triangular shape at its base (figure 5). This will be the pattern for the metal element that holds the paper leaf and to which the pin will be riveted.

5. Fold the traced triangular shape along its straightest side and draw a mirror image of the shape on the tracing paper. You should now have drawn a fan shape. Add a 1/32-inch (1 mm) margin along each side of the tracing (figure 6). (As shown in figure 7, you will loose width when the metal is bent.) Cut out the traced fan shape, leaving the slight margin.

6. Put double-sided tape on the back of the tracing and adhere it to the fine silver sheet. Use a jeweler's saw to cut out the fan shape (silver base).

7. Fold the silver base in half, and then pry it open slightly with the craft knife. Slip the paper leaf into the silver base and check the fit. The base should just enclose and cover the bottom of the leaf. Take out the paper and file the metal if necessary. File the bottom of the triangle if it is too sharp.

■ MAKING THE WIRE PINS

8. Cut a 4-inch (10.2 cm) length of the sterling silver wire. Hammer one end of the cut wire until it is wide enough to be riveted to the silver base. (Do not hammer the wire too thin, or it will become brittle.)

9. Measure and mark locations for two rivets on the hammered end of the wire, each approximately ¹⁄₁₆ inch (1.5 mm) apart. Center-punch and drill the holes for the rivets, using the 0.04-inch (0.9 mm) bit. File the end of the wire pin to a point, smooth it with sandpaper, and then polish it with a radial brush on the flexible shaft so it does not damage your clothes.

10. Place the wire pin on the silver base, and determine where the pin will be riveted to the base. (The paper leaf should be in the base.) Consider the angle and the direction of the pin, so that its curve is in harmony with the leaf's shape. Remove the paper leaf from the silver base. Tape the pin to the base in the desired position (figure 8). Make sure the pin is firmly fixed to the base. Using the two holes predrilled in the pin as guides, drill two holes into the base with the 0.04-inch (0.9 mm) bit.

11. Place a tiny bit of glue inside the open silver base. Slide the paper leaf into the base and position it correctly. Press the base shut. Let the glue dry for a few minutes. To pierce the paper, push a needle or the 0.04-inch (0.9 mm) drill bit through the two rivet holes in the metal base. Place the pin on top of the base, feed one rivet wire through the drilled holes, and rivet. Place the second wire in the second drilled hole and rivet. Sand any scratches on the leaf pin. Secure the stickpin to clothing with a catch.

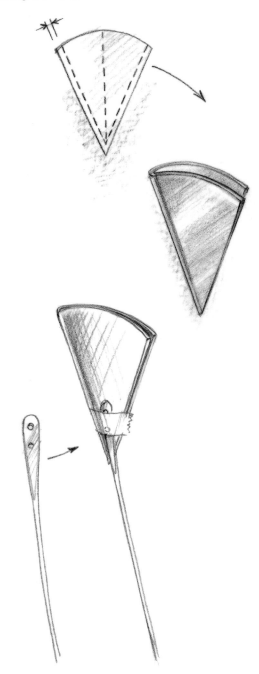

STUFFED POD PENDANT

MAKE A FASHION STATEMENT WITH A THREE-SIDED PENDANT CRAFTED BY TOPSTITCHING ON THICK PAPER, THEN LIGHTLY STUFFING IT TO PRESERVE THE GRACEFUL CURVED LINES. YOU'LL WANT TO MAKE SEVERAL VERSIONS OF THIS DESIGN TO SHOW OFF A VARIETY OF PAPER TEXTURES, COLORS, AND THREADS.

MATERIALS

Photocopied design template 1

Thick decorative paper, such as Japanese or lokta paper

Thread in contrasting or matching color for topstitching

Commercial neck wire or cord

Polyester fiberfill or cotton batting

Clasp of your choice

TOOLBOX

Single-ply cardboard

Scissors

Large binder clip

Straight pin

Ruler

Quilter's needle (smallest needle with eye large enough for thread)

Thimble

Needle tool

Tweezers

STEP BY STEP

1. Trace photocopied design template 1 onto the cardboard twice and cut out with the scissors. Place one of the cardboard templates onto the thick decorative paper and trace three times. (Some decorative papers are thinner near the edges, so avoid those areas.) Cut out the shapes and set one aside.

2. Place two of the paper shapes together in between the two cardboard templates with ⅛ inch (3 mm) of the papers sticking out the entire length of one curved side. Be careful to keep the paper shapes aligned. The cardboard creates stability while you are piercing the holes for sewing the pieces together. Hold this stack together with a large binder clip.

3. Using the straight pin, poke a hole at each pointed end, centered between the two curved edges ⅛ inch (3 mm) from each point. Starting at one end, pierce a hole every ⅛ inch (3 mm). Each hole should be approximately 1/16 inch (1.6 mm) from the curved edge of the paper. After finishing one side, repeat steps 2 and 3 for the other curved side.

4. Thread the quilter's needle with 24 inches (61 cm) of thread and double-knot the end. Put the needle in the second hole from one end. The side with the knot on it will be the inside of the pendant.

5. Hold two of the shapes to be sewed together side by side at the pointed ends where the needle is started. Make the first stitch across to the other shape into the corresponding hole second from its end. Use the thimble as needed to push the needle through the paper. Create another stitch straight across between the first two holes. There should be two stitches parallel to one another (figure 2, page 100). Always pull the thread securely, but not so much that you buckle the paper. The beginning and end of this seam will have these two extra stitches for added strength.

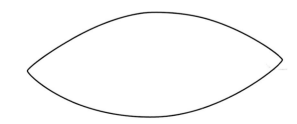

1

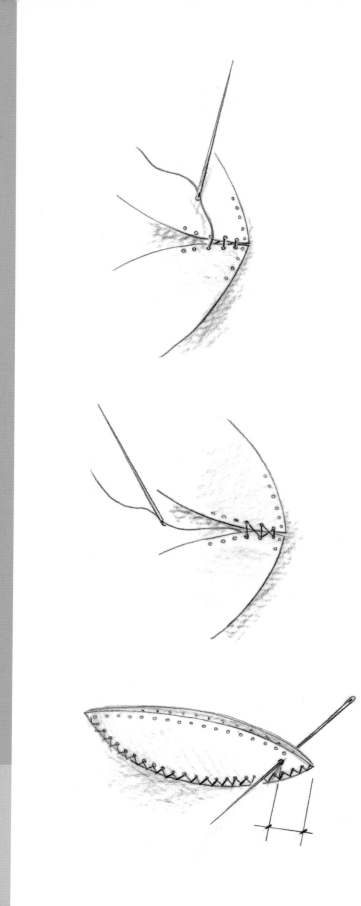

6. Next, create two diagonal stitches in between the parallel stitches. When finished with steps 5 and 6, you should have an X shape with a vertical line at each side (figure 3).

7. For ease of sewing, hold the paper structure in your left hand, if you are right-handed, with the end that is started closest to your right hand. Hold your left thumb centered over the seam, where the edges of the papers are touching (facing you), and your index finger on the back side so you are pinching both pieces of paper. (Reverse if you're left handed.) Hold the papers like this just ahead of where you are sewing, continuing to move your fingers down as you advance the seam.

8. Continue sewing in this fashion, repeating the two diagonal stitches from step 6 all the way along this seam. For a more sturdy shape, make the stitches on the back also cross over from one shape to the other. Check the reverse side frequently to make sure there is no excess thread.

9. When you get close to finishing this seam, flip the whole thing around so the end to be finished is closest to your sewing hand. When you come to the last two stitches, repeat the two parallel stitches as you did at the beginning of this seam in step 5. When you are finished with the seam, tie off the thread around a stitch on the back side. Tie around another stitch for good measure, and cut off excess thread.

10. Flatten the two sides of this shape onto one another so the inside surfaces are completely touching. Poke a hole with the needle tool where the cord or neck wire will go through the pendant (figure 4). The hole should be centered between the curves ½ inch (1.3 cm) from one of the pointed ends. Make sure the hole is large enough for the neck wire or cord that you have selected. Widen the hole if necessary, reaming it out with the needle tool.

11. Holding the third cut shape, which forms the back of the pendant, poke holes with the straight pin ⅛ inch (3 mm) from each pointed end. Then fold this shape in half lengthwise (figure 5). This will make it easier to hold inside the front portion while you sew the two back seams. Open the front sewed section and place the folded paper inside, with the folded edge going in first, so the curved edges of the front section line up with the corresponding curves of the back shape (figure 6).

12. Thread the needle with 24 inches (61 cm) of thread. Double-knot the end and thread underneath the back shape into the center hole closest to the end with the hole for the neck wire. The back seams will be sewn with the inside surfaces of the paper touching, not like the front seam, where the papers were just touching edges. Hold the two edges of the paper together tightly between your thumb on the front side, facing you, and your index finger on the back side, just ahead of where you are sewing. The first stitch will come from the hole in the back piece toward you and around the aligned edges into the first hole that is poked in the side facing you. While pushing the needle through both papers at once, you will create the hole in the back piece. Each consecutive stitch will come from where you poked it through to the other side, toward you, around the edges and back in the next hole from the front side. Continue this running stitch all down this seam. When you get to the end of the first back seam, use the hole poked in the back shape at the far end for the last stitch of this seam and first stitch of the seam for other side.

13. Flip the structure around to sew the second back seam, then continue the running stitch until you are 1 inch (2.5 cm) from being finished to leave room to stuff the inside of the pendant (figure 6). Do not sew the pendant closed until you have stuffed it. (This is an easy mistake to make and a pain to remedy.)

14. To fill the inside, pull apart small pieces of polyester fiberfill or cotton batting, roll them up and insert them into the pendant with the tweezers. Carefully push the filling down into the tip. Maintain and adjust the shape from the outside with your opposite hand while stuffing with the other. Continue filling the pendant until you reach the holes for the neck wire. Thread the neck wire or cord through both holes made in step 10. Continue stuffing the pendant, filling the tip above the neck wire but leaving unstuffed the side where you still need to sew the seam closed. Resume sewing up the side. When you are two stitches from the end, finish stuffing the pendant. Then make the last two stitches. As you put the needle into the very last stitch, push it up and through the pointed end of pendant where the three pieces of paper meet. Double-knot the thread, then push the needle back in the tip and down along the inside of the pendant until it comes out between two edges of paper at a seam. Cut off the thread and stuff the loose end inside.

15. Attach the clasp of your choice to the ends of the neck wire or cord.

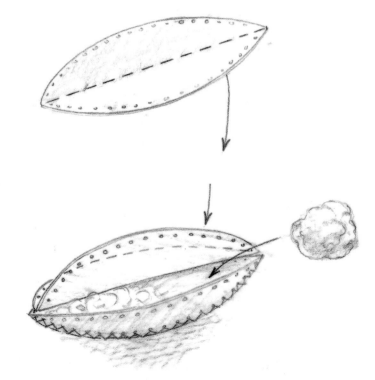

BOOK-STITCHED BRACELET

DESIGNER
K. DANA KAGRISE

THIS STUNNING BRACELET IS CREATED BY THE REPETITION OF FOLDED VELLUM CIRCLES, SEWN TOGETHER WITH A TRADITIONAL DOUBLE-ENDED NEEDLE STITCH. THE RESULT IS AN EXCEPTIONAL PIECE OF KINETIC JEWELRY THAT IS EXCITING BOTH TO VIEW AND TO WEAR.

MATERIALS

White vellum, 36 sheets, each 8½ x 11 inches
(21.6 x 27.9 cm), to yield approximately 700
2-inch (5.1 cm) circles

Card stock

Beeswax

100 percent perle cotton thread, white, one ball,
size 8

White craft glue

2 magnets, each ½ inch (1.3 cm) in diameter,
strong and thin

TOOLBOX

Circle paper punch, 2 inches (5.1 cm) in diameter

Plastic bags with zip closures

Ruler

Scissors

Permanent marker, black

2 needles, 2 or 3 inches (5.1 or 7.6 cm) long
(depending on what you have on hand and what
you prefer to handle)

Small brush (optional)

STEP BY STEP

1. Using the paper punch, punch out at least
300 circles of vellum, each measuring 2 inches
(5.1 cm) in diameter. (The designer used approximately 300 circles to make her bracelet. You will
want to have extra circles in case you damage a
few of them or to make a longer bracelet.) To help
keep track of the number of circles used, sepa-
rate them into groups of 100 and place each
group into a plastic bag with a zip closure.

2. Fold each of the paper circles in half. Keep
them divided in bags after folding.

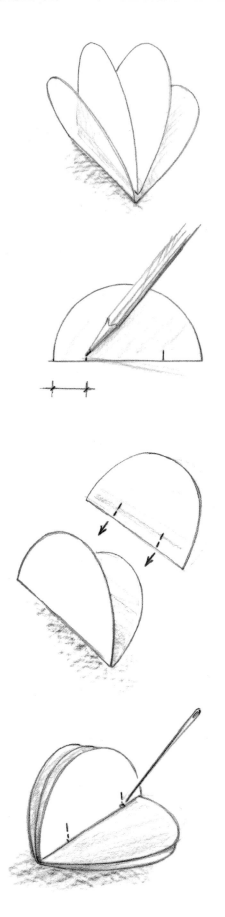

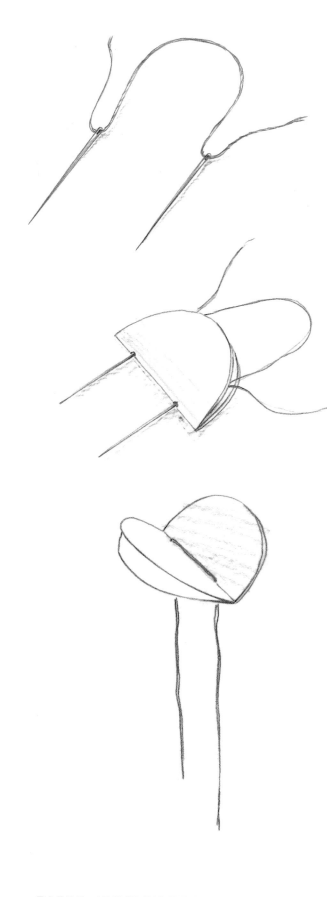

3. Prepare for punching holes in the circles by nesting two circles together (figure 1, page 103), creating a signature, and placing them on a table. (In traditional bookmaking, the nesting of papers is called a signature.)

4. To make a template for punching holes in the signatures, trace a folded circle onto a piece of sturdy cardstock paper and cut out the traced shape. Measure ⅜ inch (1 cm) in from each edge of the half-circle and mark this location with a black permanent marker or dark pencil (figure 2, page 103).

5. To punch holes for the thread to pass through, make a signature of two folded circles and insert the template into the center of the fold (figure 3, page 103). Use a needle to punch holes through the signature at each mark on the template (figure 4, page 103). Needle-punch at least 120 signatures. (It is best to punch all holes before sewing so they are even.)

■ CONSTRUCTING THE BRACELET WITH THE DOUBLE-ENDED NEEDLE STITCH

6. Cut and wax approximately 6 feet (1.83 m) of the perle cotton thread. As shown in figure 5, attach one needle at each end of the thread. From the inside of one signature, insert one needle into each hole (figure 6) and pull through. The inside of the signature should look like figure 7.

7. As shown in figure 8, place a second signature of circles on top of the first set. Insert one needle into the hole directly above it (figure 9) and pull through. Insert the second needle into the hole directly above it and pull through. Both threads should now be coming out of the inside of the second signature.

8. As shown in figure 10, take the thread on the right side and insert its needle in the left hole, bringing the thread to the outside again. Take the thread on the left side and insert its needle in the right hole, bringing the thread to the outside again.

9. Repeat steps 7 and 8 until you have sewn a set of 20 signatures. Do not cut the thread. Instead, wrap the thread around each set to keep the sewn signatures together and to keep the thread straight. Repeat this step until you have sewn and wrapped six sets of 20 signatures each.

10. To begin the process of joining the sets, first position two sets so that when they are closed and lying on their spines, the thread ends are to the right (figure 11, page 106). Re-thread the needles for the set on the left. Pretend that the set on the right is another signature to attach. Place the right-hand set on top of the left-hand set and sew them together in the same manner that you did for each of the signatures (figure 12, page 106). Repeat this process until you have

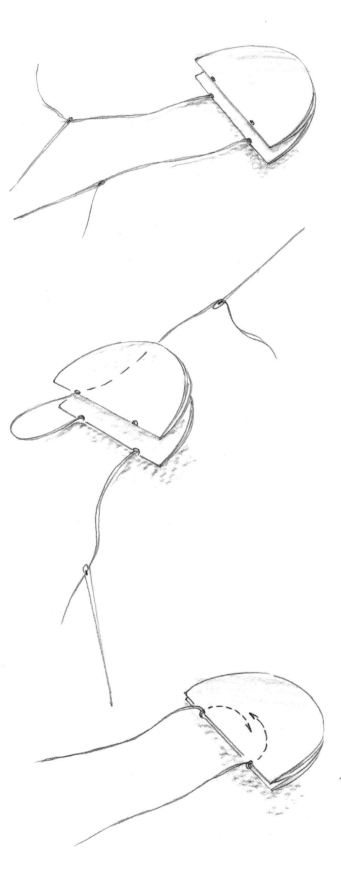

8

9

10

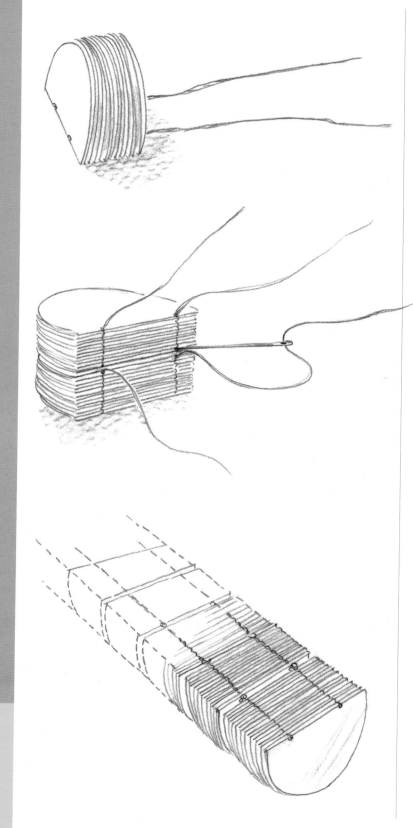

joined together all of the sets (figure 13).
(To make this process easier, you may want
to reduce the number of sets by joining two
20-signature sets to make one 40-signature set,
then joining the 40-signature sets to make the full
length of the bracelet.)

11. Once you have joined the sets together, you
no longer need the threads. Tie them off at the
base and add a dab of glue to secure the knot.
You can cut the thread at the base after the glue
has dried, or you can leave a little of the thread
sticking out on the outside of the bracelet.

12. Coat one side of a magnet with a thin layer
of glue, using your finger or a small brush. Attach
the magnet to the vellum between the fifth and
sixth signatures. Apply glue to the other side of
the magnet and press the vellum against it, sand-
wiching the magnet between the papers so that it
is glued securely in place. Repeat this process to
place the second magnet at the other end of the
bracelet.

TIANA ROEBUCK
Bun-Bun, from the *When Cousin Claira
Comes to Visit Series,* 2005
13 x 12 cm
Paper, laminated, hand cut
PHOTO © ARTIST

MIRJAM NORINDER
Phonebook Bangle (Under Construction), 2003
10 x 10 x 15 cm
Silver, telephone book pages; gilded
PHOTO © ARTIST

EUN-MEE CHUNG
Cancer Series #2, 2005
4.5 x 8 x 8 cm
Cotton linters, 18-karat gold, sterling silver,
diamond, rhodolite; cast, hand fabricated
PHOTO © ARTIST

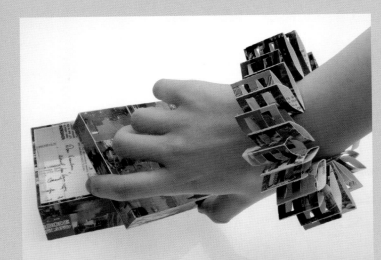

JENNACA LEIGH DAVIES
Wish You Were Here Bracelet, 2005
9 x 9 x 0.3 cm
Postcards
PHOTO © KATJA KULENKAMPFF

DESIGNER
GRACE WILLARD

KNITTED PAPER NECKLACE

Paper becomes a surprising medium for spinning, then knitting, in this inventive piece. Add matching tassel accents made from the paper cord with bell-shaped, paper-clay coverings. Shiny copper jump rings contrast with the natural colors and textures of the paper.

MATERIALS

Plain or decorative papers of your choice

Commercial paper clay (optional)

Copper jump rings (or copper wire with which to make your own)

Copper S hook fastener

TOOLBOX

Ruler

Craft knife

Scissors

Plastic bag

Towel

Card or tongue depressor

French knitting bobbin (available at craft stores) or four pegs attached to the top of a hollow tube

Small crochet hook

Drinking straw

Jeweler's pliers

Wooden dowels for making copper jump rings (optional)

Wire cutters (optional)

STEP BY STEP

1. With a pencil, lightly mark ¼ inch (6 mm) increments on the sheet of paper, leaving a 1-inch (2.5 cm) margin on both ends of the paper. Fold the paper like the letter W, so that the middle section is lower than the top and bottom. Beginning at the base of the W, carefully cut the lines with a craft knife or scissors. Make sure that you don't cut past the lines. Then, cut past the line on alternating sides to end up with one long continuous strand.

2. Place the paper strand in a plastic bag with a damp towel. Allow the paper to absorb the moisture at least overnight, if not a whole day. This will make the next few step of the project easier.

3. Allow the paper to dry. After it is dry you can begin to spin it. Tightly spin the string in one direction. As you spin the string, allow the string to be wound around a card or tongue depressor (figure 1). The tighter the string is spun the stronger it will be.

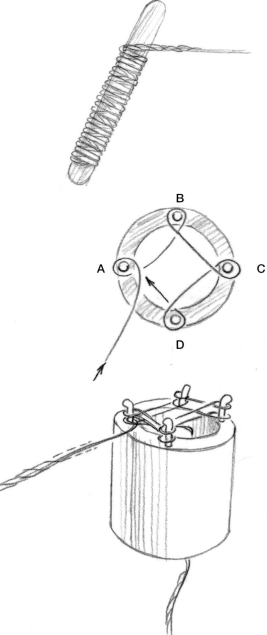

4. The next step requires a French knitting bobbin or a handmade version consisting of four pegs at the top of a hollow tube (see photo below). Thread a few inches of string through the bobbin, so that the string hangs out of the bobbin. In consecutive order, wrap the string around post A, then around post B, then around post C, and then around post D (figure 2, page 109). Repeat the process of wrapping the string around posts A, B, C, and D. There should now be two loops of string around each post (figure 3, page 109). Use a small crochet hook to lift the bottom loop over the top of the peg (figure 4). Repeat this step around, until all pegs contain only one loop.

5. Continue wrapping the string around posts A, B, C, and D, and then using the crochet hook to lift the bottom loop over the top of the peg. When the cord has reached the desired length, have one loop on each peg. With a pair of scissors, cut the cord about 5 inches (12.7 cm) from the end of the knitted piece. Carefully remove the last remaining loops from the peg (figure 5). Take the tail of the cord and thread it through each of the four loops (figure 6). Remove the piece from the knitter and pull the string tight so the loops collapse (figure 7).

6. If desired, make tassel accents to attach to the knitted necklace. Form them from a cotton pulp-kaolin mixture commercially sold as paper clay. Shape the paper clay over a removable framework that will leave a hole in the top, such as a plastic drinking straw. After the paper clay is dry, remove the straw. Group together short pieces of the paper cord and wrap a small copper wire around one end. Insert the wrapped end through the top of the paper clay form and attach to the necklace with small copper jump rings (figure 8). Make as many as you like, attaching and spacing them as desired. Use larger jump rings to attach the S-hook clasp (figure 9).

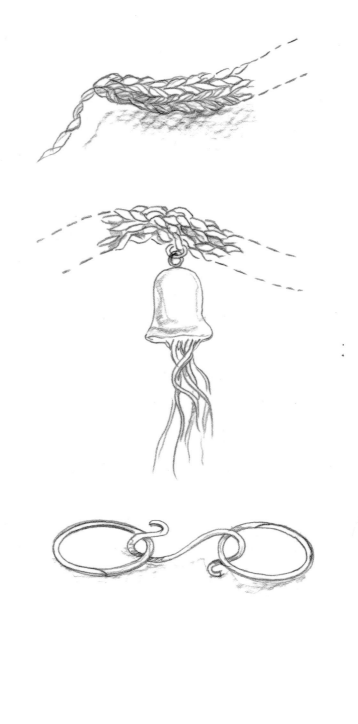

VAPOR & SMOKE EARRINGS

GOLD WIRE SOFTLY SHIMMERS BETWEEN THIN LAYERS OF WHITE TISSUE. THE PAPER IS LOOPED AND ITS ENDS RIVETED BETWEEN A FANCIFULLY CUT SHEET OF SILVER. THE EARRINGS ARE CHALLENGING TO MAKE BUT WELL WORTH THE EFFORT.

MATERIALS

Gold or gold-filled wire, 24 karat, 28 gauge

White craft glue

Tissue paper, white

Photocopied design template 4

Fine silver sheet, 28 gauge

Gold wire, 18 karat, 19 gauge

Sterling silver wire, 19 gauge

TOOLBOX

Ruler

2 smooth plastic lids

Flat paintbrush

Small sharp scissors

Jeweler's saw and saw blades

File

Flaring tool

Fine-tip permanent marker

Center punch

Steel block

Flexible shaft machine or small rotary hand tool

Drill bit, 0.04 inch (0.9 mm)

Sandpaper, 400 and 500 grit

Riveting hammer

Pliers

STEP BY STEP

1. Use your fingers to bend the gold or gold-filled wire, making two designs that are each 2½ inches (6.4 cm) long and ⅜ inch (1 cm) wide at their widest. Make sure the wire stays very flat.

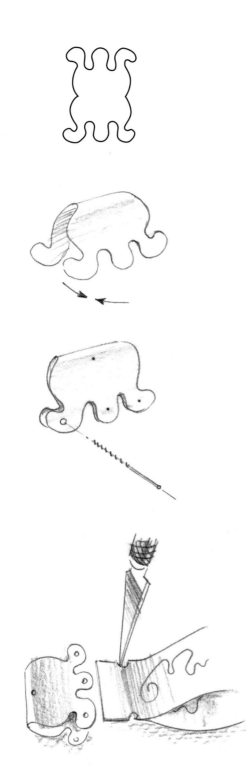

2. Make a mixture of equal parts white craft glue and water. Place one piece of tissue paper shiny side up (if it has a shiny side) on a clean plastic lid. Brush the tissue paper with the glue mixture. Place one wire design on the tissue paper (figure 1, page 113), and brush a little bit more of the glue mixture on the wire.

3. As shown in figure 2, page 113, place a second piece of tissue paper on top of the wire (shiny side down, if there is a shiny side). Use a brush to slightly moisten the top of the tissue paper with water. Using your fingers or a small flat paintbrush, lightly press the paper so the two layers bond well, especially near the wires. Push out any air bubbles that might be trapped between the two layers. If using the flat paintbrush, use gentle dabbing movements to push out the air bubbles. Be careful not to tear the paper. Very small tears don't matter too much, however, because you can have the option of choosing the best side to be the front of the earring. (If the tissue becomes very torn, take out the wire design and try again.) Leave the paper to dry flat on top of the plastic container lid.

4. Repeat steps 2 and 3 to make a second earring.

5. Measure and mark two rectangles on the tissue paper, each ⁹⁄₁₆ x 3⅜ inches (1.4 x 8.5 cm), with ³⁄₃₂ inch (2 mm) of excess paper on each side of the wire designs and ⅜ inch (1 cm) at each end. Cut out the rectangles with scissors. Gently fold the paper and wire earrings in half, forming a gentle loop. Do not press the paper at the fold. Glue the ends of the loops to each other as shown in figure 3, page 113.

6. Transfer photocopied design template 4 onto the fine silver sheet. Use a jeweler's saw to cut out the shape, and fold it as shown in figure 5. Check that the front and back of the metal form match, and make adjustments as needed by filing and using the flaring tool. Repeat this step to make a second, identical silver form.

7. Using a fine-tip permanent marker, mark locations on both pieces of silver for the three wire-rivet holes and for the ear wire. With the center punch, dimple the four holes in each silver piece, then drill each hole with a 0.04-inch (0.9 mm) bit (figure 6). File and sand both silver pieces.

8. Open the silver shapes, slide in the paper, and check if anything needs to be altered. Remove the paper and cut as needed (figure 7). Place a tiny dot of white craft glue on the top of the paper and insert it into the folded metal part. Fold the sides of the silver piece together so the paper is held securely. Let the glue dry a few minutes. Push the 0.04-inch (0.9 mm) bit through the drilled holes to pierce the paper and make it easier for the rivets to go through (figure 8, A). Repeat for the second earring.

9. Measure the thickness of the folded silver where it is to be riveted. Add ¹⁄₁₆ inch (1.8 mm) to this amount, then cut six pieces of the 18-karat gold wire to this measurement. Make a wire rivet in the lower drilled holes on both earrings (figure 8, B). If needed, sand the silver to erase any hammering marks, but take care not to damage the paper.

10. Cut two pieces of the sterling silver wire, each 1¾ inches (4.4 cm) long. Bend the sterling silver wire into an L shape. Thread the small end of the L through the hole for the ear wire and round it up into a loop with pliers (figure 9). Bend the long end of the wire to form a hook (figure 10). Repeat to make another ear wire for the second earring.

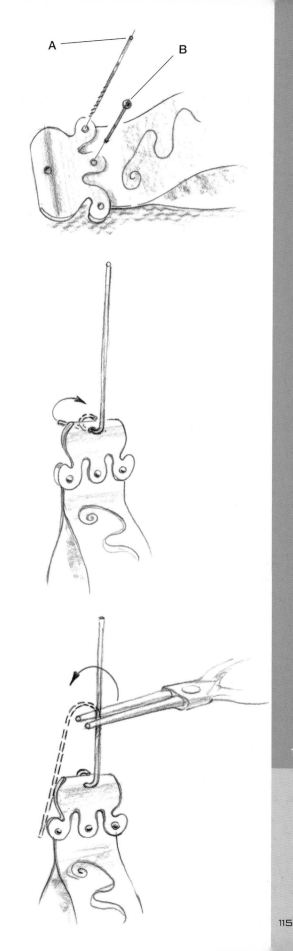

ACCORDION PENDANT

RICHLY TEXTURED NEPALESE LOKTA PAPER IS THE STAR OF THIS DESIGN. TWO CONTRASTING COLORS OF PAPER IN WARM EARTH TONES ARE FOLDED AND SECURED WITH CLEAR ACRYLIC AND STERLING SILVER WIRE TO CREATE A STRUCTURED PAPER PENDANT.

MATERIALS

2 sheets of thick paper such as lokta, each 20 x 30 inches (50.8 x 76.2 cm), in contrasting colors

Sheet of clear acrylic, $\frac{1}{32}$-inch (0.08 mm) thick

Sterling silver wire, 18 gauge, 6 inches (15.2 cm)

Commercial cord or neck chain of your choice

TOOLBOX

Ruler

Scissors

White craft glue or rubber cement

2 large binder clips

Small, motorized cutting tool

Drill bits, $\frac{1}{16}$ inch (1.6 mm) and $\frac{3}{32}$ inch (2.4 mm)

Wood block for drilling

Permanent marker, ultra fine tip

Jeweler's saw and saw blades

Large flat file

Green scrub pad

2 pairs of pliers

Dowel, $\frac{3}{8}$ inch (9.5 mm) in diameter

Wire cutters

STEP BY STEP

1. Trim off the uneven edge of one sheet of paper by drawing a straight line down the 30-inch (76.2 cm) side and using scissors to cut off the uneven edge. Repeat with the other sheet of paper.

2. At the top and bottom of one sheet of paper, mark $\frac{15}{16}$ inch (2.3 cm) inside the straight edge you just made. With the ruler, draw a line to mark a strip that is $\frac{15}{16}$ inch (2.3 cm) wide the entire length of the sheet. Cut off the strip and erase any pencil marks.

3. Repeat step 2 with the second sheet of paper, except mark and cut a strip that is $\frac{9}{16}$ inch (1.4 cm) from the straight edge.

4. Cut across one end of each strip so it is straight. Lay the cut end of the narrow strip over the cut end of the wide strip so the pieces form a large L shape with the wide strip vertical and the narrow strip horizontal (figure 1, page 118). Glue these ends with a small amount of white craft glue or rubber cement and let dry.

5. Fold the wide strip back upon itself, toward you, making sure that the edges of the paper align (figure 2, page 118). Make a sharp crease by running your thumbnail along it. Think of this strip as folding first South, then North, over and over in between the folds of the other strip.

6. Fold the narrow strip back on itself (figure 3, page 118). Make sure that the edges of the papers line up in the stack you are forming. Make the new fold crisp by running your thumbnail along it. Think of this strip as folding first West, then East, in between the folds of the other strip.

7. It is easy to hold this in your hands while folding. Repeat steps 5 and 6 until you fold all of the narrow strip of paper. Cut the ends of each strip so they meet up with the corresponding edge of the last complete fold. Glue these last two pieces of paper together and let dry.

8. Measuring from one end of the folded structure, mark the middle of the rectangle with a pencil, checking with the ruler to make sure that it is the middle in both directions. Hold the folded structure firmly, keeping it tightly together, and attach a binder clip on both short sides of the stack. Using the small, motorized cutting tool with the $\frac{1}{16}$-inch (1.6 mm) drill bit, hold the

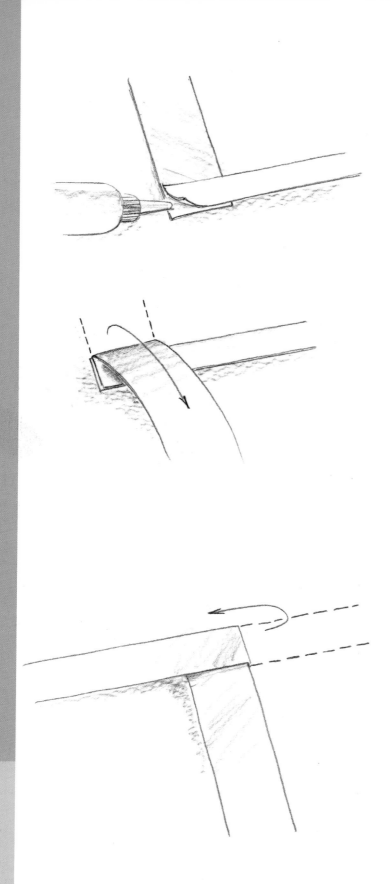

structure firmly on a scrap of wood and slowly drill straight down all the way through the paper (figure 4).

9. Remove the binder clips. Hold a piece of the clear acrylic (with the protective film still in place) on top of the folded structure. Trace around the paper with the ultra-fine tip permanent marker, being careful not to mark on the paper. Repeat for the bottom side of the folded structure. Cut out both acrylic shapes with the jewelry saw on a bench pin.

10. Hold the acrylic pieces over the corresponding sides of the paper structure, looking down at the paper through the acrylic, and mark the positions of the drilled holes on both pieces. While holding the acrylic piece on the scrap wood, drill a hole in the bottom piece with the $\frac{1}{16}$-inch (1.6 mm) bit on the spot marked. Change to the $\frac{3}{32}$-inch (2.4 mm) bit and drill the top piece of acrylic on the marked spot. Remove the protective film and file all edges of the acrylic rectangles with the large flat file. Rub the edges of acrylic with the green scrub pad.

11. Place the 6-inch (15.2 cm) piece of sterling silver wire in the pliers, leaving $\frac{1}{2}$ inch (1.3 cm) sticking out of the top of the pliers (figure 5). With your fingers, bend this end over the pliers, creating a 90-degree bend (figure 6). File a rounded point on the short end of the wire with a flat file. Make another 90-degree bend in the wire $\frac{1}{4}$ inch (6 mm) from the filed end. The wire should have a squared U shape on one end, with the other end completely straight (figure 7, page 120).

12. Thread the bottom piece of the acrylic, then the folded paper structure, and then the top piece of the acrylic onto the straight end of the wire. Double-check to make sure that all pieces are in the correct order and that the edges of the acrylic line up with the edges of the folded paper.

13. Mark the spot where the tip of the U-shaped end comes back and touches the bottom piece of acrylic. This mark can be next to or diagonal from the drilled hole, as long as it is no closer than ¼ inch (6 mm) from the closest edge. This will be a second hole to lock the pendant in place and prevent it from turning on the central wire. Unthread the acrylic and paper from the wire.

14. Drill a hole with a ¹⁄₁₆-inch (1.6 mm) bit on the marked spot on the bottom piece of acrylic. Mark the position of this new hole on the bottom of the paper structure. Bind the paper again with the binder clips and drill approximately ¼ inch (6 mm) into the bottom of the paper structure.

15. Rethread the whole assembly, making sure that the U-shaped end fits up into the second drilled hole. Now place the paper structure on the wire and decide how open or closed down you want the structure for the pendant to be. (The pendant shown has the folds very open.) Add the top piece of acrylic (the one with the larger drilled hole), and push the paper down out of the way. Place the central wire in the pliers at the point where you want the bale to be with the end of the wire sticking above the pliers. Fold the wire over and create a 90-degree angle (figure 8, page 120). Make sure you have the pliers parallel to the wider section of the paper, so that when you bend the wire it points out over the wider section. This will ensure the bale is in the correct orientation.

16. Place the ⅜-inch (9.5 mm) dowel over the corner of the 90-degree angle and wrap the loose end of the wire around the dowel until it forms a complete circle, coming to the point where the wire was bent (figure 9, page 120). Remove the dowel.

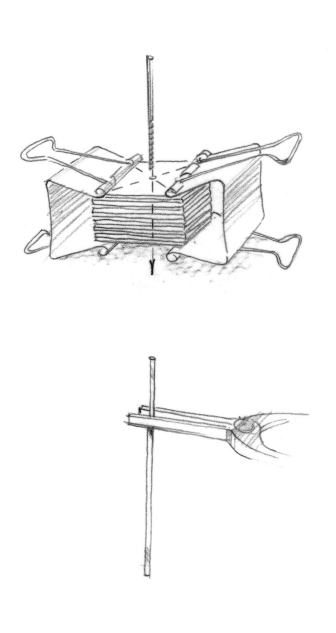

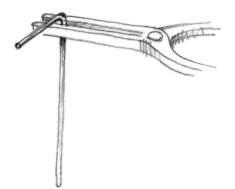

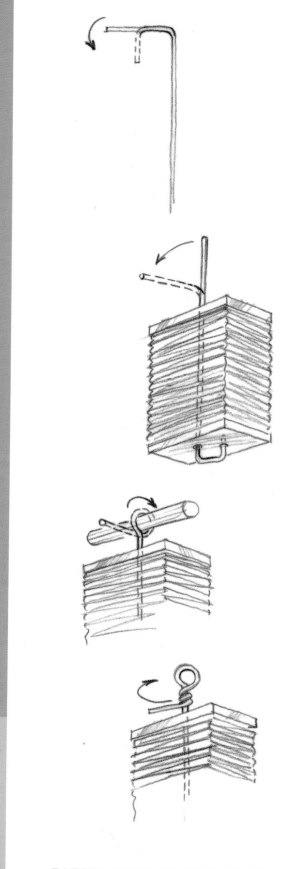

17. Grab the circle along its width with one pair of pliers, continuing to make sure that the paper structure is pushed down so you will have room to wrap the loose end of the wire. It is easier to wrap wire if you have a long piece to hold onto, so do not cut it yet. Starting immediately below the circle, tightly wrap the loose end around the straight part of the wire three times (figure 10). Cut the wire with the wire cutters ⅛ inch (3 mm) from the wrapped part. With the file, round the end of the wire. While holding the circle with one of the pliers, place the jaws of the other pliers around the wrapped section and finish wrapping as you turn the structure in your hands. Pull up the top piece of acrylic so it fits over the wrapped section. You may have to twist the acrylic piece around in a circle, and then adjust the paper.

18. Using the circle created in step 16 as the bale, thread the pendant on a commercial neck chain or cord of your choice.

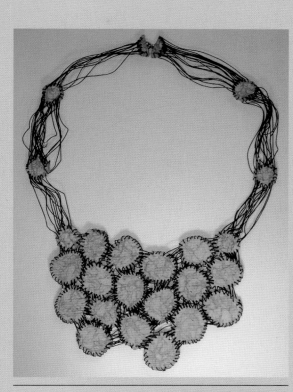

SILJE BERGSVIK
Untitled, 2005
19 x 10.5 x 0.4 cm
Silk paper, silver, freshwater pearl;
hand fabricated, papier-mâché
PHOTO © ARTIST

SAM THO DUONG
Verstecktes Rot, 2000
52 x 10 cm
Tags, leather thread;
singed, bent, strung
PHOTOS © PETRA JASCHKE
COURTESY OF BAUHAUS ARCHIV,
MUSEUM BERLIN

MASUMI KATAOKA
Untitled, 2002
8 x 8 x 8 cm
Cardboard, sterling silver; glued, fabricated
PHOTO © ARTIST

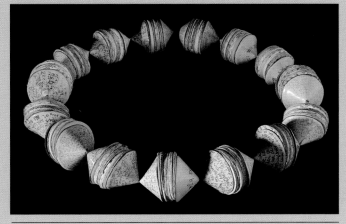

INGEBORG VANDAMME
Diary-Necklace, 1995
Length, 25 cm
Copper, enamel, graphite, book pages
PHOTO © HENNIE VAN BEEK

MULBERRY BANGLES

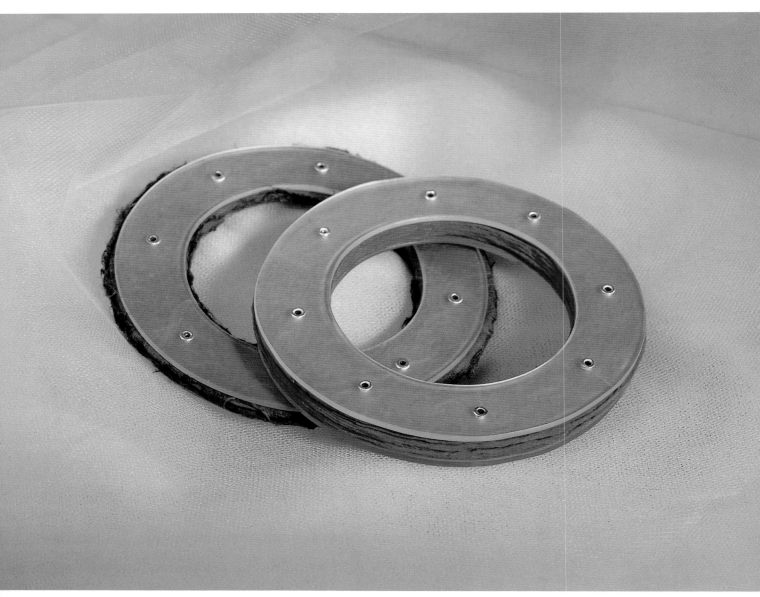

BRIGHT RED PAPERS ARE LAYERED BETWEEN ACRYLIC RINGS, AND THEN RIVETED TOGETHER TO MAKE THESE EXCEPTIONAL BRACELETS. VARY THE LOOK BY LAYERING DIFFERENT COLORS OF PAPER, OR BY MODIFYING THE DIMENSIONS AND SHAPE OF THE ACRYLIC.

MATERIALS

Acrylic sheet, 8 x 10 inches (20.3 x 25.4 cm), 0.08 inch (2.03 mm) thick, protective film left on both sides

Decorative papers (designer used red mulberry and reversible red and black unryu)

Aluminum tubing, ³⁄₃₂ inch (2.4 mm) in diameter

TOOLBOX

Compass

Single-ply cardboard

Ruler

Scissors

Permanent marker, ultra-fine tip

Jeweler's saw and saw blades

Wood block

Flexible shaft machine or small rotary hand tool

Drill bits, ¹⁄₁₆ inch (1.6 mm) and ³⁄₃₂ (2.4 mm)

Large half-round file, single cut

Green scrub pad

Small sponge, 1 x 2 inches (2.5 x 5.1 cm) (optional)

Duct tape

Needle tool

Round needle file

Flaring tool

Hammer

Steel block

NOTES

■ The inside diameters of bangle bracelets vary by size.

Small bangle = 2¼ inches (5.7 cm)

Medium bangle = 2½ inches (6.4 cm)

Large bangle = 2¾ inches (7 cm)

■ The instructions are for making one bangle bracelet.

STEP BY STEP

■ MAKING A TEMPLATE FOR THE BRACELET

1. Determine what size bangle bracelet you want to make and note its interior diameter. Use a compass to mark a circle on the single-ply cardboard that corresponds to the interior diameter.

2. To make your bracelet the same width as the one shown, increase the compass measurement ¾ inch (1.9 cm). Using the same center point as the circle drawn in step 1, mark the larger circle on the cardboard with the compass.

3. Cut out the cardboard template with scissors and try it on for size. If the sizing is incorrect, alter your measurements and make a new template. Now is the time to make sure you have the dimensions you prefer.

■ CUTTING & FINISHING THE ACRYLIC CIRCLES

4. Use the ultra-fine point marker to trace the cardboard template onto the protective film that covers the acrylic sheet. With a jeweler's saw, cut out the acrylic along the outer marked line, taking care to hold the blade straight up and down. Repeat this step to trace and cut out a second acrylic circle.

5. Place one acrylic circle on a piece of scrap wood. Using the flexible shaft or small rotary tool with the ¹⁄₁₆-inch (1.6 mm) bit, drill a hole inside the inner marked line of the acrylic circle. Thread the saw blade through the drilled hole and saw out the interior circle slowly, turning the acrylic as the saw advances. Repeat this step for the second acrylic circle.

6. Use the curved side of the half-round file to clean up the interior sawed edge on both acrylic pieces. As you push the file away from you, slowly curve it to one side, making a sweeping motion forward and sideways. This motion will maintain the curve of the interior circle.

7. Use the file to bevel a 45-degree angle on both interior edges of the acrylic so it will be more comfortable to wear. Try on each bangle. If they are too small, file their inner circles until they fit. File the outside edges of both acrylic pieces using the flat side of the file. Once smooth, rub the green scrub pad back and forth along all edges to finish.

■ MAKING THE PAPER CIRCLES

Note: The thicker the bracelet you construct, the more difficult it is to rivet. The thin bracelet uses six pieces of solid red paper with cut edges and three pieces of red and black paper with torn edges. The 12 paper layers in the thicker bracelet were cut with scissors. Use these structures or modify as desired.

8. Option A: To make paper circles with cut edges, lay one acrylic disc on the paper. Trace the disc with a pencil and cut it out with scissors, poking a hole in the inner circle to start the cut. Repeat this step for each paper layer that has cut edges. Erase any pencil marks.

Option B: To make paper circles with torn edges, start with a square of paper that is larger than the acrylic discs. Hold the paper over a disc and push the excess paper edges over the outer rim of the disc. Wet the small sponge and rub it on a section of the paper that is wrapped over the rim. Place your thumb on top of the paper next to the dampened section. Use your other hand to pull the dampened paper outward, creating a torn edge. Repeat this process as you slowly rotate the ring of paper and acrylic. Rewet the sponge as needed. You can let the paper dry out if it gets too wet.

To tear the inner circle, first use scissors to cut out a circle in the very center of the paper. Hold the paper over one of the acrylic discs. Use the sponge to wet sections of the paper that extend past the inner edge of the acrylic. Pull the damp paper down and in, away from the acrylic disc's inner edge. Repeat this process for each layer of paper with torn edges. Lay all paper discs flat and let dry.

■ BINDING & DRILLING THE DISCS

9. Place the two acrylic discs directly on top of each other and tape together with four ½ x 3-inch (1.3 x 7.6 cm) pieces of duct tape. Wrap the first piece of tape from the front side of the discs around the outside edge and up through the center hole until you use up the tape. The pieces should be immovable.

10. Visualize the acrylic disc as a clock face with the first piece of wrapped tape at 12 o'clock. Wrap the remaining pieces of tape at 6 o'clock, 3 o'clock, and 9 o'clock. Make a dot with a permanent marker to the right of each piece of tape, making sure they are centered on the width of the acrylic. Mark four additional points on the disc, each one halfway between the original points and centered on the width of the acryliic.

11. Hold the taped and marked acrylic discs on the scrap wood. Place the 3/32-inch (2.4 mm) bit in the flexible shaft or rotary tool. Holding the bit straight up and down, slowly and smoothly drill holes at each of the eight marks. Leave the tape on the acrylic discs.

■ FINISHING THE BRACELET

12. Stack the dry paper discs in the desired order, making sure to turn the proper side out on the first and last pieces of paper.

13. Tear a section of the protective film off one side of the acrylic discs and place a small piece of duct tape next to one of the drilled holes. Flip over the acrylic disc, tear off more protective film and put another piece of tape next to the corresponding drilled hole. (This helps you put the discs back together with matching drilled holes aligned.)

14. Remove the duct tape that is binding the two acrylic discs. Place the paper layers between the acrylic discs, making sure the drilled holes match by lining up the duct tape squares.

15. Remove all remaining protective film from the acrylic. Create a uniform frosted look on the acrylic by rubbing all the flat surfaces in overlapping circles with the green scrub pad. This finish prevents the acrylic from looking scratched.

16. While firmly holding the acrylic and paper layers together, poke a hole with a needle tool through one of the drilled holes, piercing each paper layer and exiting the drilled hole on the second disc. Wiggle the needle tool back and forth to widen the hole, and then file out excess paper with the round needle file.

17. While tightly holding all of the acrylic and paper discs together, measure the thickness of the bracelet in millimeters. Add 5/32 inch (4 mm) to this measurement. Measure and mark a piece of aluminum tubing to this length, and cut it out with a jeweler's saw. File the cut end of the tube rivet flat.

18. Insert the tube rivet in the hole and work it through to the other side. (If this is difficult, insert the point of a needle tool in the tubing and push with the handle or use an awl.) Adjust the tubing so that equal amounts stick out on each side of the acrylic.

19. Hold the bracelet over the steel block, making sure one end of the tube rivet touches the block. Position the flaring tool on the top end of the tubing, and tap the tool several times with a hammer. Flip the bracelet over, equalize the amount of tubing sticking out on each side, and flare the rivet. Repeat this sequence of events, flipping, equalizing, and flaring, until the tube ends are flared and the rivet is stuck in the hole. Then, tap directly on the tube rivet with the hammer to flatten out the flare. Flip the bracelet over and repeat. Continue until the rivet is uniformly flattened. **Note:** The paper does not offer much resistance. If you continue to hammer on the rivet, it will get tighter and tighter. When setting the rivets, just tap enough to make a small head appear on each side.

20. Cut seven additional tube rivets the same length as the first one, and sand the cut ends. Turn the first rivet to 12 o'clock and prepare the drilled hole at 6 o'clock for riveting. Set the second rivet. Prepare the hole and set the third rivet at 3 o'clock. Prepare the hole and set the fourth rivet at 9 o'clock. The bracelet should no longer be able to shift from side to side, so you can set the remaining four rivets in any order.

ORIGAMI CRANE COCKTAIL RING

A SYMBOL OF HEALTH, HAPPINESS, AND PEACE IN THE JAPANESE CULTURE, THE CRANE BECOMES A UNIQUE ORIGAMI COCKTAIL RING WITH THE ADDITION OF A SIMPLE BAND. CHOOSE BRIGHT COLORS OF ORIGAMI PAPER OR MESH TO MAKE THIS CLASSIC FOLDED PAPER DESIGN.

MATERIALS

Origami paper or mesh in colors of your choice

Sewing thread in colors to match the origami paper or mesh

TOOLBOX

Table top or other smooth, flat working surface

Needle

STEP BY STEP

■ FOLDING THE ORIGAMI BAND

1. Start with a square piece of origami paper or mesh (figure 1).

2. Fold the paper or mesh square into a rectangle (figure 2).

3. Fold the rectangle again (figure 3A), and again (figure 3B), to make the band.

4. Fold one end of the band to make a flap (figure 4) that is approximately ¾ inch (1.9 cm) long.

5. Fold over the end of the flap into the band, creating another tight crease that is approximately ¼ inch (6 mm) from the end of the band (figure 5). The band should now have two creases. Place the band on the table with the folded flap facing down.

6. Take the unfolded end and fold it under the band at a 90-degree angle (figure 6, page 128). (The exact length to fold depends on the ring size you want to make.)

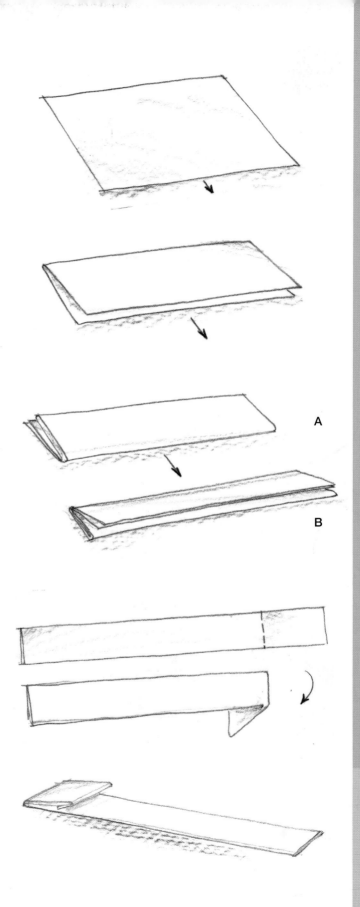

A

B

7. Fold the straight end of the band over the back of the horizontal piece (figure 7).

8. Roll the end with the folded flap back and around in a circle to meet the folds (figure 8).

9. Fold the straight end of the band around the ring.

10. Tuck the end of the flap under the end piece that was just wrapped (figure 9). The flap should fit snugly and hold the ring in place.

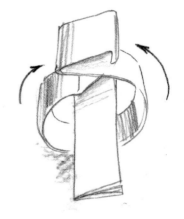

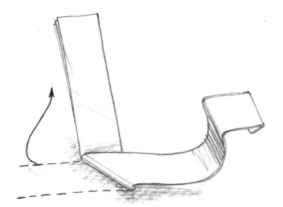

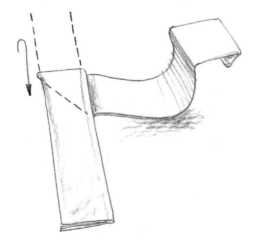

■ FOLDING THE ORIGAMI CRANE

12. Start with a square piece of origami paper or mesh. (This piece can match or contrast with the origami band.) Fold the paper diagonally, joining opposite corners (figure 10).

13. Make a second diagonal fold (figure 11) to create a vertical crease, and then unfold this step.

14. Fold in the upper right and the upper left edges to meet the centerline (figure 12). Crease, and then unfold both folds (figure 13).

15. Following the preliminary creases, inside reverse fold both sides (figure 14, page 130). You will need to partially open the figure and to reverse the creases on top to tuck the corners inside the flap.

16. Fold the lower sides of the left and right flaps to the centerline (figure 15, page 130). Unfold the left and right flaps (figure 16, page 130).

17. Using an inside reverse fold, tuck the corners of the left and right flaps inside (figure 17, page 130). In order to slip in the side corner, you must reverse the creases on top and lift up the top sheet.

18. Repeat steps 5 and 6 on the reverse side to form the base of the bird (figure 18, page 130).

19. Fold up the front and rear flaps of the bird as shown in figure 19, page 130.

20. On the front and the back of the bird, fold in the lower sides to meet the centerline (figure 20, page 130).

21. Book-fold the front and the back of the bird (figure 21, page 130).

22. Fold up the front flap as far as it will go,

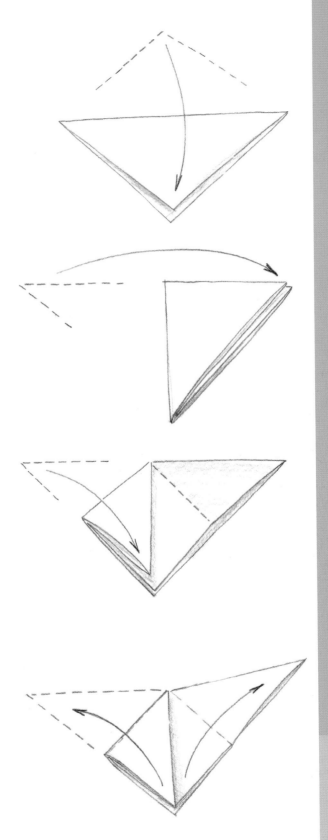

10

11

12

13

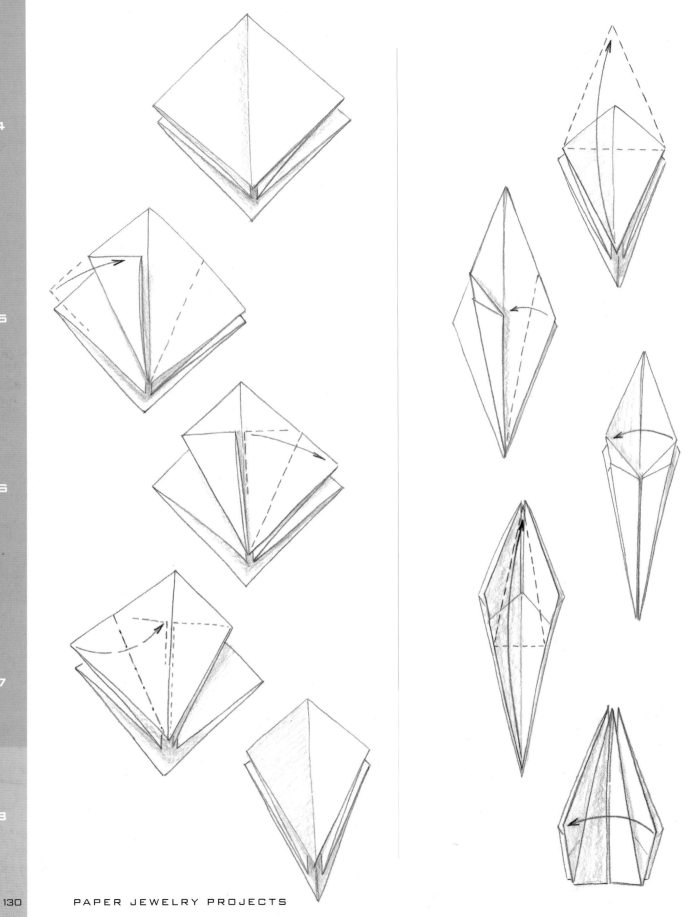

and then fold up the back flap as far as it will go (figure 22). One flap becomes the neck, and the other becomes the tail.

23. Book-fold the front and back of the form to reveal the wider wings (figure 23).

24. Gently pull down the neck and tail of the bird until they are flush with the edges of the body (figure 24).

25. Inside reverse fold one-third of the neck to form the head of the bird (figure 25).

26. Gently pull down the wings to a horizontal position (figure 26). Figure 27 shows the completed crane.

27. Stitch the crane to the ring with the needle and thread.

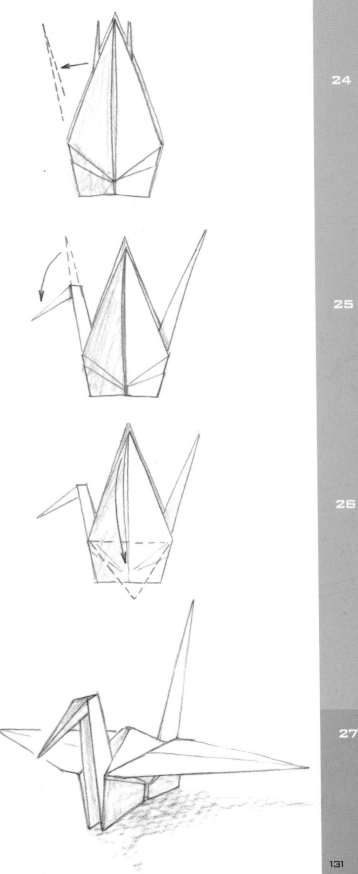

YOON JEE JUNG
Happy Meal, 2005
Left, 3 x 10.5 x 3.2 cm; right, each 3.5 x 3.5 x 2 cm
Rice paper, Korean paper, paint, mixed media; cut, rolled
PHOTO © STUDIO MUNCH

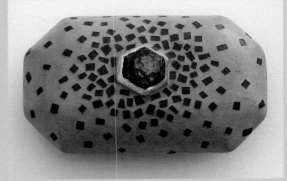

SILKE TREKEL
Untitled, 2005
7.5 x 4.2 x 1.8 cm
Balsa wood, rice paper, silver, sapphire
crystals, gold foil, paint; laminated
PHOTO © ARTIST

YUN HEE KIM
Untitled, 2005
10 x 10 x 5 cm
Korean paper, string; dyed,
hand fabricated
PHOTO © MYUNG-WOOK HUH

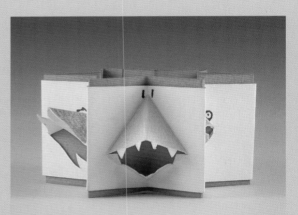

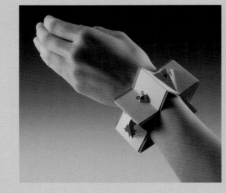

JENNIFER HALVORSON
Pop-Up Monsters, 2006
4.4 x 10.2 x 10.2 cm
Card stock, drawing paper,
colored pencil, marker
PHOTOS © ARTIST

ILANA RABINOVICH-SLONIM
Just Having Fun, 2003
Closed, 7 x 27 x 27 cm; open, 7 x 68 x 7 cm
Paper rope, paper ribbon, glue;
hand fabricated, rolled, woven
PHOTO © EREZ AURAHAM

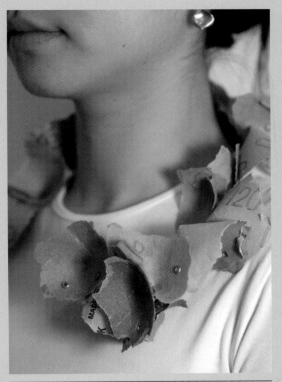

KIT BURKE-SMITH
Grit, 2005
8 x 20 x 30 cm
Used sandpaper, eyelets; riveted
PHOTO © LAUREN SIMON

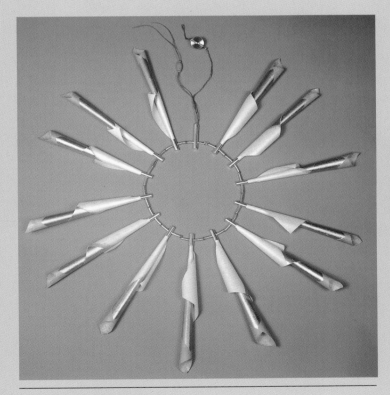

NICOLE JACQUARD
Yo-Yo's Necklace, 2001
0.5 x 46 cm diameter
Joss paper, silver, 22-karat gold, silk,
crystal, glass; hand fabricated, folded
PHOTO © KEVIN MONTAGUE

RALLOU KATSARI
Dilima, 2006
7 x 6.5 x 0.7 cm
Yellow paper, glue powder, silver; papier-mâché
PHOTO © FEDERICO CAVICCHIOLI

GALLERY

JULIE SCALISE STUMPF
Pink Fur Muff, 2005
20 x 40 x 20 cm
Handmade silk paper, velvet; coptic binding

ZOË JAY VENESS
...1,2,3,5..., 2005
Length, 38 cm
Paper, 9-karat gold, 10-karat gold, nylon-coated
stainless steel cable; hand fabricated

RENEÉ ZETTLE-STERLING
Memory Collar, 2005
Variable dimensions
Paper doilies soaked in coffee,
thread, beads, plastic

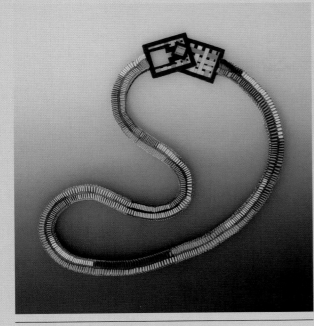

KAREN J. LAUSENG
Untitled, 2006
230 x 80 x 10 cm
Cardboard, quilling paper; woven

NICOLE BSULLAK
Untitled Fibula, 1998
3.8 x 5.1 cm
Sterling silver, old letters, resin

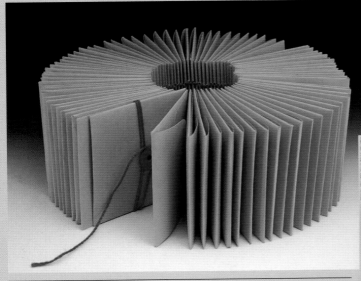

K. DANA KAGRISE
Someone Else's Vacation, 2005
5.1 x 15.2 x 15.2 cm
Manila envelopes, cotton thread, vintage slides,
aluminum rivet; cut, hand fabricated, stitched

GALLERY

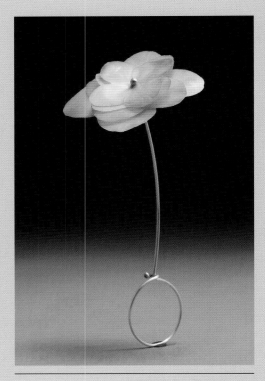

SALLY A. HODOVANIC
Untitled, 2006
30.5 x 30.5 x 10.2 cm
Paper lanterns, beads, string
PHOTO © BRIAN W. LUCAS

CARRIE GARROTT
Paper Hydrangea Ring, 2006
7.5 x 2.5 x 2.5 cm
Vellum, sterling silver, beeswax; laser printed
PHOTO © ARTIST

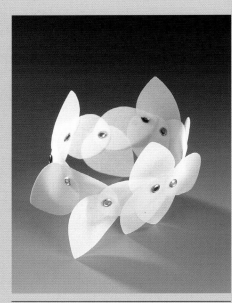

PAULINE DENNIS
Untitled, 2006
6.4 x 7.6 x 7.6 cm
Tissue paper, nickel, copper;
hand fabricated, laminated, layered, riveted
PHOTO © JEFF SABO

EDWARD LANE MCCARTNEY
Stones, 2004
Each, 3 x 5 x 7 cm
Sterling silver, papier-mâché, paint, lacquer
PHOTOS © JACK ZILKER

SUSAN R. EWING
*Serie Arquitectonica: Broken
Window Brooch #2*, 1987
2.5 x 5 x 5 cm
Bristol board, graphite, white glue;
hand cut, drawn, fabricated
PHOTO © JEFFREY SABO

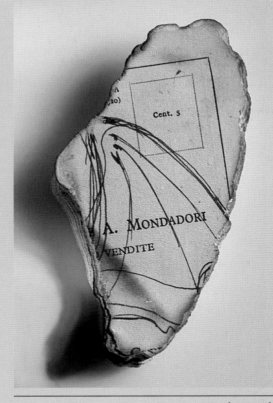

FLÓRA VÁGI
Untitled, 2005
7 x 13.5 x 1.5 cm
Book pages, cold enamel;
hand fabricated, sawed, painted
PHOTO © FEDERICO CAVICCHIOLI

PAUL LEATHERS
Slidemount Brooch, 1987
5 x 5 x 0.6 cm
Slide mount, watercolor paper, sumi ink,
bronze, stainless steel
PHOTO © ARTIST

ASTRID BARNDÄL
Angels Book I + II, 2006
Each, 7 x 7 x 2 cm
Tracing paper, 23-karat gold leaf, thermoplastic
PHOTO © ARTIST
COURTESY OF VELVET DA VINCI, SAN FRANCISCO, CA

GALLERY

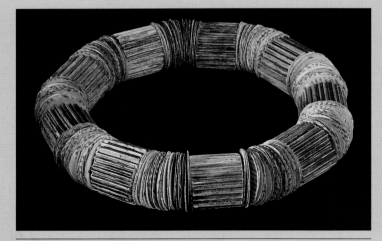

INGEBORG VANDAMME
Plant-Necklace, 1996
Length, 26 cm
Plant, book pages, paraffin
PHOTO © HENNIE VAN BEEK

GEOFF RIGGLE
Royal Flush, 2006
14 cm in diameter
Playing cards, sterling silver;
hand fabricated, riveted
PHOTO © JEFFREY SABO

KATE CATHEY
Winter Birch Bracelet, 2006
8.9 x 10 x 10 cm
Copper, gampi tissue, beeswax, charcoal,
pastel, pearls, thread; formed, fabricated,
sgraffito, encaustic, sewed, oxidized
PHOTO © JOHN CARLANO

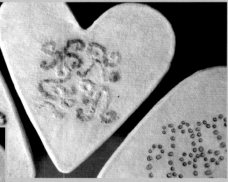

FRANCINE HAYWOOD
Coeurs Occultes, 2001
5 x 5 cm
Tissue paper, toilet paper, sterling silver,
steel pin, gold leaf, 24-karat gold wire, fine
silver wire, hair; laminated, fabricated
PHOTOS © AMANDA MCKITTRICK

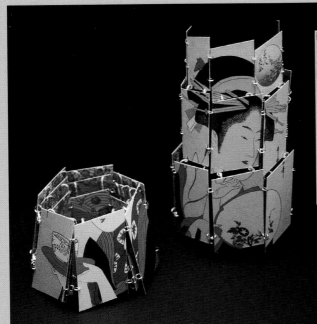

TAIKO MAI ROSKOTHEN
Shy Ladies, 2006
Left, 6 x 7.5 x 7.5 cm; right, 14.5 x 7.5 x 7.5 cm
Japanese paper, postcard, copper wire, glue,
sterling silver wire; hand fabricated

ELISA DEVAL
Untitled, 2005
15 x 15.5 x 6.5 cm
Newsprint, tissue paper, glue, wood;
papier-mâché, hand fabricated

SUN KYOUNG KIM
Winter Breeze, 2006
75 x 50 x 25 cm
Paper rope, thread; twisted

GALLERY

WALTER CHEN
Bracelet, 2006
6.5 x 12.5 cm diameter
Parchment card, rice paper,
silicone thread; dyed, folded

MI-MI MOSCOW
Kiss of Fire, 2005
5.5 x 10 x 9.8 cm
Paper, textile

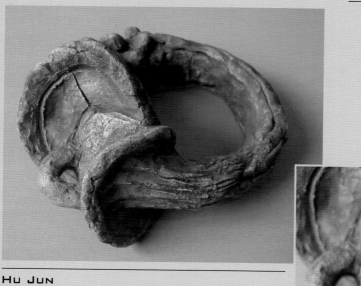

HU JUN
Untitled, 2005
7 x 12 x 14 cm
Paper pulp, paint; hand fabricated

CAROL-LYNN SWOL
Bracelet, 2006
5.1 x 16.5 x 15.2 cm
Stacked Tyvek

SASKIA BOSTELMANN
Six Meters of Jewelry, 2006
75 x 15 x 3 cm
Paper, 18-karat gold wire,
paint; folded, rolled, glued

KATE SHORT
Accordion Book Necklace, 2004
Open, 14 x 43.2 x 6.4 cm; closed, 14 x 14 x 6.4 cm
Lokta paper, batik paper, thin card stock, satin ribbon, linen
bookbinding thread, bookboard; hand bound

YOKO SHIMIZU
Untitled, 2005
38 cm in diameter
Rice paper, resin, silver

DESIGNER PROFILES

JAMES BOVÉ earned a BFA from West Chester University in Pennsylvania in 1993. His Teacher Certification and MFA were granted by Edinboro University of Pennsylvania in 1998. He has shown his artwork both nationally and internationally. James resides in Washington, Pennsylvania, and teaches at California University of Pennsylvania as an assistant professor.

SARAH KATE BURGESS teaches at Interlochen Arts Academy. She graduated magna cum laude with a BFA in Jewelry/Metals from the University of Massachusetts at Dartmouth. Her MFA in Metalsmithing was granted by Cranbrook Academy of Art. She pursued a residency at Oregon College of Art and Crafts, was a visiting critic at Pacific Northwest College of Art, and had a Studio Assistantship at Arrowmont School for Art and Craft. She is a co-founder of Takt Kunstprojektraum, Berlin, Germany.

CANDIE COOPER received degrees in Fine Arts and Art Education from Purdue University. She currently lives in Shanghai, China, where she works as a studio jeweler and designer. Candie's passion lies in creating jewelry from mixed materials. Her jewelry has been exhibited in the United States and Europe.

ÖZAY EMERT was born in 1975 in Merzifon, Turkey. She received her bachelor's degree from Mimar Sinan Fine Arts University in Istanbul, and is currently a master's candidate at HDK, School of Design and Crafts of Goteborg University, Sweden. Besides being a jewelry artist, she also taught sculpture to elementary school students. For the brooch in this book, she was inspired by the millions of butterflies that congregate at the Sakarya Bridge in Turkey every year in mid-July.

YAEL FRIEDMAN holds a Jewelry Technician diploma from the Revere Academy in San Francisco, California; a diploma in Graphic Design from the Vital School of Design in Tel-Aviv, Israel; and a BFA from the Jewelry Department of the Bezalel Academy of Arts in Jerusalem, Israel. Her work has sold in galleries in Israel and the United States for the last 10 years. She has also exhibited in Europe.

JOANNA GOLLBERG is a studio artist in Asheville, North Carolina. She enjoys making many types of metal work, especially jewelry, which she exhibits at galleries and craft fairs throughout the United States. Joanna is a graduate of the Fashion Institute of Technology with a degree in jewelry design and has taught workshops at the Penland School of Crafts and the John C. Campbell Folk School. She is the author of three Lark books, *Making Metal Jewelry*, *Creative Metal Crafts*, and *The Art & Craft of Making Jewelry*.

ELIZABETH HAKE first took a jewelry class in 1993, at the Arrowmont School of Arts and Crafts, and it inspired her to return to college to receive a BFA in Metalsmithing/Jewelry from Northern Michigan University in 1996. In 2002 and 2003, she returned to Arrowmont as an Artist-in-Residence. She lives in North Carolina, where she operates a studio full-time; she also teaches workshops at the John C. Campbell Folk School and Arrowmont.

FRANCINE HAYWOOD was born in France. She studied Chinese art and archeology before moving to Asia; while in Japan, she was introduced to paper as a means of artistic expression. After studying jewelry design in Australia, she decided to experiment with paper jewelry making. In her work, she combines paper, metal, and embroidery techniques to create ephemeral but wearable pieces that evoke life's fragile beauty and the passing of time.

DOROTHEA HOSOM is a studio metalsmith particularly interested in enamel and mixed-media jewelry. She received a BA from the University of Cincinnati, and an MA from Long Island University. Her work has been exhibited at the Cape Cod Museum of Art; in Trashformations East at the Fuller Craft Museum; and in the Enamelist Society 10th Biennial International Juried Exhibition. It also appeared in the book *500 Brooches*. dhosom@whoi.edu

K. DANA KAGRISE earned undergraduate degrees—a BFA in Metals and a BS in Art Education—from Miami University, Ohio, in 2002. She recently graduated with a master's degree in Art Education from the University of Illinois, Urbana-Champaign. While a student there, she taught a course in the metals program and assisted with courses in the art education program. Dana currently teaches art to students at the middle and high school level in the New Albany-Plain Local school district in Ohio. In addition to receiving the Emerging Artist Award from Ohio Designer Craftsmen and other awards, Dana has had work published in *1000 Rings*, *Fabulous Jewelry from Found Objects*, and *500 Bracelets*.

CLAUDIA LEE is a fiber artist, papermaker, and workshop leader. She lives in Liberty, Tennessee, where she owns and operates Liberty Paper Mill, a working and teaching facility. She is the author of *Papermaking*.

KELLY NYE graduated from Columbus College of Art & Design in 2006, receiving a BFA in Fine Arts with a focus on jewelry and metalsmithing. She plans to attend graduate school and hopes to teach metalsmithing in the future. Her current body of jewelry is a marriage of sterling silver and silicone rubbers to form large, colorful rings in a pop style. These rings are created with the intention to look obnoxious, but they're fun to wear!

D. LYNN REED (DONNA) was initially interested in jewelry as adornment, then as an art form, and later as a means of communication. She is a self-taught jewelry artist and silversmith who owns and operates her own studio in Columbus, Ohio. Donna exhibits locally via galleries and art shows. She has taught jewelry, metal, collage, and polymer clay classes through bead shops, guild associations, and the Ohio Craft Museum, among other places. Her jewelry designs and class schedules are available at modernjewelryart.com.

MARJORIE SCHICK is an internationally recognized artist whose work has been exhibited in museums and galleries around the world. It is also part of the permanent collections of such institutions as the Victoria and Albert Museum in London, the Royal Museum of the National Museums of Scotland, and the National Museum of Modern Art in Kyoto, Japan. She received her undergraduate degree in Art Education from the University of Wisconsin-Madison, then studied under master jeweler Alma Eikerman at Indiana University-Bloomington, obtaining her MFA from there in 1966. Schick has been a member of the Pittsburg State University faculty since 1967. Her work has been featured in many national and international books and magazines, including on the cover of *Metalsmith* magazine. In 2004, she was interviewed for the Smithsonian Institution's Archives of American Art Oral History Program as part of the Nanette L. Laitman Documentation Project for Craft and Decorative Arts in America. In recognition of her distinguished artistic career, she was named a Fellow of the American Craft Council in both 2000 and 2002, and also received the Kansas Governor's Artist Award. Marjorie served as the juror for the book *500 Necklaces*.

YOKO SEKINO-BOVÉ was born in Osaka, Japan in 1970. She earned a BFA in Graphic Design from Musashino Art University in Tokyo. After moving to the United States, Yoko attended the graduate program at the University of Oklahoma, earning an MFA degree in Ceramics. Yoko's work is widely exhibited across the nation, and her work was featured in the volume *500 Cups*. Yoko currently works in her home studio in Washington, Pennsylvania.

CAROLINA TELL is a Swedish jewelry artist who experiments with different materials such as paper and textiles. She received her MFA in Jewelry Design at the School of Design and Crafts at Göteborg University in 2005. Carolina has shown her work in galleries and museums across Sweden and at the Stockholm Art Fair. In 2005, she participated in The Loan Exhibition about contemporary Swedish silver at The International Art and Design Fair in New York.

KYOKO URINO was born in Tochigi, Japan. In addition to holding a diploma from Central Saint Martins College of Art, London, she received an MA from New York State University and an MFA from Southern Illinois University at Carbondale. Kyoko's national and international exhibitions include "Contemporary Japanese Jewelry" at the Crafts Council, London; "Nature and Time" International Jewelry Competition, Society for Goldsmiths' Art, Germany; and Merit Awards at the Associated Artists Gallery in Carbondale, Illinois.

GRACE WILLARD received her BFA in studio arts from Columbus College of Art & Design in 2005. While mainly focusing on drawing, she studied both papermaking and jewelry in addition to achieving a minor in art history. She currently resides in Columbus, Ohio; she exhibits locally and throughout the region.

CYNTHIA B. WULLER received her BFA from the School of the Art Institute of Chicago. She currently creates jewelry, accessories, and clothing. Her love of shapes and textural contrasts shows in all her pieces.

INDEX

ACKNOWLEDGMENTS

I am grateful to the 19 artists who gave of their time and talent to produce projects for this book. Thanks for your imagination, skill, and generosity. I am indebted to the gallery artists who shared images of their creations. Your ideas and innovations are truly inspiring.

The Lark Books team that worked on this book is tremendously gifted. Special thanks go to editorial contributors Nathalie Mornu, Dawn Dillingham, and Delores Gosnell, and to art contributors Dana Irwin, Lance Wille, Barbara Zaretsky, and Jeff Hamilton. Deborah Morgenthal's wisdom, guidance, and encouragement have always elevated my work, and I appreciate her steadfast commitment to quality.

Vivian Rothe worked enthusiastically and methodically to mold this book into shape. Thank you for your editorial insight and passion. The stellar photography of Stewart O'Shields is a welcome addition to any book, and I am fortunate to feature his work. Olivier Rollins's pencil illustrations and Orrin Lundgren's computer templates are superlative. Thank you for providing these important elements.

Thanks to the art galleries, organizations, teachers, schools, and publications that vigorously support, promote, and advance the field of contemporary jewelry.

INDEX OF ARTISTS

NOTES ON SUPPLIERS

Usually, the supplies you need for making the projects in Lark books can be found at your local craft supply store, discount mart, home improvement center, or retail shop relevant to the topic of the book. Occasionally, however, you may need to buy materials or tools from specialty suppliers. In order to provide you with the most up-to-date information, we have created a list of suppliers on our website, which we update on a regular basis. Visit us at www.larkbooks.com, click on "Craft Supply Sources," and then click on the relevant topic. You will find numerous companies listed with their web address and/or mailing address and phone number.